HOW TO START A
MAIL ORDER BUSINESS

Other **21ST CENTURY ENTREPRENEUR** *Titles*
from Avon Books

HOW TO OPEN A FRANCHISE BUSINESS
by Mike Powers

HOW TO OPEN YOUR OWN STORE
by Michael Antoniak

HOW TO START A HOME BUSINESS
by Michael Antoniak

HOW TO START A RETIREMENT BUSINESS
by Jacqueline K. Powers

HOW TO START A SERVICE BUSINESS
by Ben Chant and Melissa Morgan

The 21st Century
ENTREPRENEUR

HOW TO START A
MAIL ORDER BUSINESS

MIKE POWERS

A Third Millennium Press Book

AVON BOOKS  NEW YORK

VISIT OUR WEBSITE AT
http://AvonBooks.com

THE 21ST CENTURY ENTREPRENEUR: HOW TO START A MAIL ORDER
BUSINESS is an original publication of Avon Books. This work has never before
appeared in book form.

AVON BOOKS
A division of
The Hearst Corporation
1350 Avenue of the Americas
New York, New York 10019

Copyright © 1996 by Third Millennium Press, Inc., Stephen M. Pollan, and Mike
Powers
Published by arrangement with Third Millennium Press, Inc.
Library of Congress Catalog Card Number: 96-24601
ISBN: 0-380-78446-7

Library of Congress Cataloging in Publication Data:

Powers, Mike.
   How to start a mail order business / by Mike Powers.
      p.   cm.—(The 21st century entrepreneur)
"A Third Millennium Press book."
Includes bibliographical references and index.
1. Mail-order   business—United   States.   2.   New   business   enterprises—United
States.   I. Title   II. Series.
HF5466.P683   1996   96-24601
658.8'72—dc20   CIP

First Avon Books Trade Printing: December 1996

AVON TRADEMARK REG. U.S. PAT. OFF. AND IN OTHER COUNTRIES, MARCA REGISTRADA, HECHO
EN U.S.A.

Printed in the U.S.A.

OPM   10   9   8   7   6   5   4   3   2   1

Thanks to Mark Levine and Stephen Pollan for their friendship and advice, and to Jim Spitznagel for giving me a glimpse into the future of the mail-order business.

❧CONTENTS❧

Chapter 1: The Perfect Time to Go into Business   1
Chapter 2: Nothing But Growth Ahead   15
Chapter 3: Are You Ready to Run Your Own Business? 34
Chapter 4: The 12 Rules for Doing It Cheaply   51
Chapter 5: Financing Your Business   65
Chapter 6: What Will You Sell?   77
Chapter 7: Testing the Market   96
Chapter 8: Setting Up Your Business   114
Chapter 9: Creating a Business Plan   143
Chapter 10: Getting Your Customers' Attention   153
Chapter 11: The Electronic Storefront   179
Chapter 12: The Nuts and Bolts Stuff   198
Chapter 13: Fun and Profit   225

Index   235

HOW TO START A
MAIL ORDER BUSINESS

1

THE PERFECT TIME
TO GO INTO BUSINESS

So you want to go into business for yourself. I don't blame you. Working for yourself is the most rewarding way I can think of to make a living. When you run your own business, you alone are responsible for the success you create. You make all the decisions and chart your own path. By virtue of your own hard work, you take the credit—and the profit—for your success.

But working for yourself is not always a bed of roses. Just as you reap the credit for success, you're also responsible if the business fails. Self-employment also has some inherent risks, the biggest of which is what makes it attractive in the first place—you're on your own. In addition, the hours can be grueling and irregular, making family life and personal relationships difficult. It often doesn't have the benefits and "perks" that come with corporate employment. And the risk of financial disaster is always just around the corner. Still, most business owners will tell you it's the only way to fly.

THE LURE OF SMALL BUSINESSES

Small businesses have characteristics that will always make them attractive. From a consumer's point of view, they're usually more pleasant to deal with than large businesses. For one thing, they can offer personalized service of the highest quality.

1

Don't you enjoy walking into a store where the people know you by name? It means you have a special relationship with the owner and the employees and can count on being treated special. It also means you'll keep coming back.

As an example, look at the small family-owned grocery store not far from my house. It's run by the son of the founder, and several family members work there part-time. I pass it almost every time I go out and stop there at least once a day to pick up the papers or buy milk or bread or some other item we need.

When we first moved here, I immediately discovered the store and began to stop in regularly. Within a week they all knew my name and began treating me like an old friend. Now when I go in I know I'll end up hanging around, talking about one thing or another. If I forget my wallet I can put my purchases on a tab. There's a sign on the counter—No Checks Accepted. I can write checks. They even gave my daughter a part-time job while she was in high school. It all seems like such insignificant stuff, but it really makes a difference in how I feel about the business.

Small businesses are also more flexible and quicker to adapt to change than large businesses are. When market or consumer trends require a quick adjustment, a small business can turn on a dime to react. By contrast, a large corporation will turn the corner with all the speed and agility of the *Queen Mary*.

As we approach the end of the 20th century, small businesses are being created at a pace not seen for decades. During the 1980s, more than 600,000 new businesses were created each year. The 1990s have been called the decade of the small business by many business experts. Women and minorities are starting businesses at a record rate. This is no accident. Working for yourself makes especially good sense these days. Let's examine some of the reasons for the resurgence of the small business and some of the options open to the 21st Century entrepreneur.

CORPORATIONS ARE DOWNSIZING

One of the biggest reasons that small businesses are growing is the downsizing of America's corporations. When many parents of the baby boom generation entered the workforce, they could go to work for a big company and almost always count on spending the rest of their lives working there, if they chose. There was a sense of loyalty to the company, and that sense of loyalty was returned; companies went out of their way to take care of their people. America's economy was thriving, our big corporations were growing by leaps and bounds, their workers' jobs were secure, and the future showed nothing but promise.

But those days are over. Over the last fifteen years, foreign competition and cheap overseas labor have smacked American companies square in the face and awakened us to the fact that our seemingly untouchable corporate Goliaths are indeed vulnerable to these overseas Davids. "Made in Japan," a tag that consumers laughed at in the sixties, elicited consumer confidence by the eighties. Products from other Asian nations soon attracted the same respect.

One of the industries most severely affected by foreign competition was the automobile industry. By the end of the seventies, the Chrysler Corporation, sagging under a deluge of Japanese imports that were affordable, well-built, and fun to drive, was teetering on the edge of extinction. Several other car companies were close behind. Our clothing industry suffered when many of its jobs moved to Asia, with its lure of cheap labor. The steel industry watched in dismay as its foundries fell silent, brought to their knees by foreign competition. The electronics industry was also hit hard. Today you can no longer buy a television that has been manufactured by an American-owned company.

To compete in the new world economy, corporations throughout the United States have had to tighten their belts to avoid drowning in a sea of red ink. Their goal is to become lean and mean and keep profits—and the price of their stock—as high as possible. As a result, they're laying off employees faster than ever before; in 1994, white-collar unemployment surpassed blue-collar unemployment for the first time in history as 516,000 people were jettisoned from corporate payrolls. Coincidentally, while this book was being written, AT&T announced it was "reinventing" itself by splitting into three separate companies. Wall Street loved the news, and AT&T stock soared. Less happy were the 40,000 people who discovered they were losing their jobs.

Companies also are merging with one another in an effort to boost profits. Just a few weeks before the AT&T announcement, two of the nation's biggest banks, Chemical Bank and Chase Manhattan Bank, announced the largest merger in the industry's history. Again, it was great news for shareholders as the banks' stocks took off. When the merger is complete, it will have created the nation's largest bank. But 12,000 people will have lost their jobs in the process. The most unfortunate of them will find themselves in late career with salary needs that make them unattractive to most potential employers.

Downsizing Means New Opportunities

It's not surprising, therefore, that many of these corporate casualties are starting small businesses. Some are staying in the same fields they were in during their corporate lives, starting consulting firms (if they can find clients) or service firms in accounting, payroll management, human resources, and other areas.

There are good opportunities for them. The rash of corporate downsizing in the late 1980s and the 1990s has created a new buzzword in American business—*outsourcing,* which means that companies hire outside firms to take care of some of the tasks their employees used to do. Outsourcing frees the companies of employee-associated costs such as FICA, health insurance, pension plans, and the like. In many cases, former employees have gone right back to work for the companies who laid them off, only this time as independent contractors rather than as employees. And this time, the former employee, not the corporation, is responsible for his taxes and insurance.

But many other former corporate workers are venturing into fields that are entirely new to them. They're finally indulging their true interests, starting bookstores, cooking supply stores, art galleries, restaurants, golf shops, and all sorts of other businesses. Though few of them will make the kind of money they made in their previous jobs, most don't care. They've discovered that the pleasures of being your own boss and the freedom that comes with owning your own business are worth the sacrifices they may have to make because of a reduced income.

Another thing they're discovering (and something you and any other new entrepreneur will discover) is that running a small business is a lot more complicated than they thought. Rather than having the tidy set of responsibilities you have in corporate life, when you run your own business you wear every hat, from CEO to janitor. It keeps you on your toes and makes you learn quickly. Those who don't fail quickly.

WE'RE NOW A SERVICE ECONOMY

Because of the decline of corporate America, particularly in manufacturing, we're rapidly becoming a service-based economy. Business services, home and lawn services, catering, child-care, commercial cleaning, automobile services, home improvements—the list of potential businesses is virtually endless.

Economists predict nothing but future growth for service businesses. Over the years, as our economy has expanded, personal spending on services has soared. Today, more disposable dollars are spent on services than on durable goods. This trend should continue for the foreseeable future.

The reason for this is simple: Americans are busy people. Most come from two-income families with hectic schedules. They're willing to pay for services that provide them with the time to relax and enjoy their downtime. The market for leisure-time "experiences" is also growing. People pay a lot of money for classes, hobbies, vacations, and health clubs, in addition to having their lawns mowed and their homes cleaned.

Take a simple thing like eating. Obviously, the oldest service business related to eating is the restaurant. The next oldest is probably catering. But as society changed and people had even less time to cook other ways of servicing hungry Americans arose.

Ray Kroc saw the need for take-out fast food; now McDonald's, Wendy's, Burger King and other fast-food joints are an integral part of the American landscape. More and more restaurants offer delivery and takeout. I even know of a woman who will come to your home and, at the end of the day, leave your freezer stocked with a month's worth of tasty and nutritious dinners. All you have to do after a hard day at work is come home and pop one in the microwave. The next day, there's usually enough left over for lunch.

The bottom line with service businesses is simple. If enough people don't want to do something and are willing to pay good money to have it done for them, you have a business opportunity before you.

HOME-BASED BUSINESSES ARE FLOURISHING

Home is no longer just where the heart is; it's frequently where the job is as well. As I mentioned before, quite a few people who have been cast adrift by big corporations have started consulting businesses or other services to take advantage of "outsourcing" opportunities. Many of them are working at home or at least using their home as a base of operations.

But they're not the only ones who have discovered the luxuries and benefits of the home office. Many people who still work for large corporations also now work at home, connected to the office and their clients by computers, modems, fax machines, and cellular phones. It's a trend that's growing because corporations have found that, in most cases, employees are happier and more productive when they work at least part of the time at home. The elimination of the daily commute gives them more time at home and allows them to become more involved in family and community activities.

It also makes sense to the bottom line. Cornell University's Frank Becker, a professor of design and environmental analysis, advises companies around the world on efficient office design. He says that many companies are discovering that allowing their employees to work at home reduces the amount of office space they need to lease. Rather than providing each employee with his or her own desk, many are turning to what Becker calls the "non-territorial office." Under this system, as many as four or five employees will share a workstation, keeping their personal belongings and work materials in lockers and getting them out when they show up at the office. In the meantime, says Becker, the office is becoming more of a base where people gather for meetings and to socialize.

For the budding entrepreneur, working at home merits serious consideration. Obviously, some businesses require a storefront or an office. But many others, particularly service businesses and, as we'll see later in this book, mail-order businesses, are tailor-made for home operation. (For more information on home-based businesses, see Michael Antoniak's *How to Start a Home Business,* another book in The 21st Century Entrepreneur series.)

EXAMINING YOUR OPTIONS

When you're thinking about starting a business, two big questions always loom above all others: What business do I want to be in? and How much money do I have to invest? In today's business world, there are many choices. Here are some of your options.

Start a Service Business

If you are an entrepreneur with big dreams and a modest budget, starting a service business is an excellent option. It allows you to put your talents to work by offering your customers a service you think you can provide at a profit. For example, you might start a home remodeling business, a painting business, or an automotive services business. If you have expertise in nutrition and exercise, you might become a personal trainer for fitness buffs. If you have a background in business, you might offer your talents as a consultant to other businesses or businesspeople.

Service businesses are inexpensive and easy to start up because *you* are the product. Therefore, you don't have to tie up a lot of money in inventory. Also, you may be providing the service at the customer's home or place of business. So rather than needing a storefront, your service business could be operated out of your home or from a car or van. You won't need to hire employees, either, at least not at the outset of your business. (If you need employees later, it's a good sign. It means your business is expanding.) The only real investment you might need to make is for equipment. Many service businesses can be started for less than ten thousand dollars. Some can be started for only a few *hundred* dollars.

There are downsides to service businesses, however. For one thing, they're extremely competitive, so you need to provide the best service you possibly can. You need to be a self-starter, organized, focused, and you need to make sure you either show up when you tell your customers you're going to be there or are there when they show up at your place. Service businesses aren't for procrastinators or people who have trouble motivating themselves. (We'll take a look at your personal characteristics and how suited you are to business ownership in chapter 3.)

Another problem with service businesses is that they often require you to work when everyone else is playing. Consider a catering business. Your customers are people throwing parties, weddings, business dinners, and other social gatherings. Most of them will be in the evening and on weekends. If you don't like working this type of schedule, you may be unhappy.

(Another book in The 21st Century Entrepreneur series, *How to Start a Service Business* by Ben Chant and Melissa Morgan, can give you more information on service businesses.)

START A RETAIL BUSINESS

For those entrepreneurs with more capital, opening a retail store is a traditionally popular strategy. Retailing allows you to immerse yourself in the things you love—books, gourmet foods, sporting goods, clothing, electronics—by selling them directly to the consumer. And if you enjoy customer contact and don't mind the long hours, it's a great way to make a living.

A downside of retailing is the cost. You'll need more capital because you'll need a place to do business. That means buying or leasing a storefront or building. You'll need inventory, store fixtures, one or more computers, the appropriate software, and a wide variety of supplies. You'll probably need at least one employee and some money for advertising and promotion. It's also a pretty good idea to have a substantial financial cushion beneath you to help you weather the uncertainty of your first few years in business. For these reasons, setting up even the most modest retail business will usually cost anywhere from ten to twenty thousand dollars. Depending on the size of the business and the type of product you sell, you may need several hundred thousand dollars or even several million dollars.

Another negative of retailing is the long hours. You don't make money when the doors are locked, so most retail stores are open seven days a week and, except for Sunday, twelve or more hours a day. This means that either you have to be there or you need to hire people to run the show while you get some time off.

Retailing also means constant contact with the public. Dealing with the public is not always a bucket of chuckles. Most of your customers will be delightful people who are a pleasure to work with. But, human nature being what it is, you'll also have some customers who are just miserable human beings. You have to be prepared to keep a smile on your face and treat them courteously when what you'd really like to do is throw them out the door. When you run a retail operation, the last thing you need is someone running around saying terrible things about you.

(Michael Antoniak's *How to Open Your Own Store,* another book in The 21st Century Entrepreneur series, will give you good advice on getting started in retailing.)

Buy an Existing Business

Some entrepreneurs choose to buy an existing business. This has some advantages. The biggest plus is that the business has already established a track record. If it's been around for a number of years and shows a consistent history of profitability and growth, it's less likely to fail than a brand new business.

It has an established clientele, it's known in the community, and people know what they'll see when they walk through the doors. When you buy it, you hit the ground running.

The downside is you'll pay for the business's successful track record. It's called goodwill. In addition to assuming the costs associated with starting a brand-new business, you're paying the seller a premium for the success and longevity he achieved. Of course, if the business continues to perform well and grow under your ownership, you can probably recoup your investment when you sell it. If you've really done well, you might be able to get a lot more for it than you paid. Still, buying a business is expensive. If you don't have much capital, it's really not an option.

BUY A FRANCHISE

Some people pursue their dreams by buying a franchise. If they buy wisely, this gives them a head start on the person who starts a business from scratch or buys an existing business: when you buy a franchise, you're buying a tried and tested business system that gives you a product that's in demand and a successful method of marketing that product. The person who sells you the franchise—the franchisor—has created his business system through years of trial and error and is now reaping the rewards of his own hard work by selling you the secrets that made him successful.

There's no question that franchises are a very attractive option for the 21st Century entrepreneur. The industry has been growing by leaps and bounds for the last twenty years. There are more than 550,000 franchised businesses in the United States. With sales approaching $800 billion, they account for more than a third of all retail sales. If franchises continue to grow at the pace they've grown at in recent years, by the turn of the century they'll account for nearly half of all retail sales and ring up more than *$1 trillion* a year in business.

One downside of buying a franchise is the cost. Not only do you have the same costs associated with starting a business from scratch or buying an existing business but you'll also have to pay the franchisor an initial fee for the franchise, as well as a certain percentage of your gross sales each month in royalties the entire time you own your franchise. Franchise fees can range from several thousand dollars to several hundred thousand dollars, depending on the size of the business, and royalty fees are usually from five to seven percent. Sometimes another percent or two is tacked on each month to cover advertising costs. That's a big chunk of change to be giving up each month.

Another problem with franchising is the fact that there are a lot of people trying to sell franchises who either aren't ready to act as responsible franchisors or who are just plain trying to rip people off. It's always been a fairly looney industry, and although it's much more regulated today than ten or twenty years ago, you can still get taken if you're not careful.

This is not to say that there aren't good franchise opportunities available. There are several thousand very good companies out there. But for some reason, people think that if they buy a franchise they're buying a sure thing, and that's just not the way it works. Buying a franchise requires that you thoroughly investigate the franchisor and the company beforehand to make sure you're getting what you're paying for. Doing it right can take months, if not years. (To learn more about franchising and how to approach the purchase of a franchise, look at another book I've written in The 21st Century Entrepreneur series, *How to Open a Franchise Business*.)

THE LURE OF MAIL ORDER

Like franchising (and for many of the same reasons), mail order is one of the premier growth industries for the 21st Century, and it is one of the best bets for entrepreneurial success.

A quick look at the numbers illustrates just how quickly the industry is growing. Between 1980 and 1994, retail mail-order sales in the United States grew from around $28 billion to approximately $123 billion. Business-to-business mail-order sales were even more impressive, going from $18.5 billion to more than $130 billion. Most analysts feel this growth will continue for the foreseeable future.

More than 15,000 businesses now sell their goods and services through catalogs. Others operate solely through classified ads in selected magazines and newspapers. The rapid proliferation of home computers and the growing interest in electronic communication is inspiring many others to set up "electronic storefronts" on the Internet.

Mail-order businesses run the gamut from mom-and-pop businesses operating out of their basements or garages to retailing giants like J. C. Penney and Montgomery Ward. Some are operated part-time by people who want to supplement their income from other jobs. Others are full-time endeavors that are experiencing healthy growth and profits. They sell everything imaginable and offer a full range of prices. Whether you want a $15,000 diamond-and-ruby necklace or a $15 zircon-and-glass knockoff, you can find it in a mail order catalog.

The reasons for the growth and popularity of mail order are a combination of demographics, societal changes, and technological breakthroughs. For consumers, the main attraction is the convenience. They can purchase a wide range of merchandise by simply spending a few minutes on the phone or, increasingly, the computer. A day or two later, their purchases arrive. It's quick and it's easy.

For you and other entrepreneurs, operating a mail-order business combines the best of both retail and service with few of the hassles. You're operating a retail business, but one with little face-to-face customer contact. And you're operating a service business in the sense that you're providing a huge convenience to your consumers—saving them time and simplifying their lives. And as we'll see in the next chapter, that may be just about the most valuable thing you can offer people today.

WHERE DO WE GO FROM HERE?

Perhaps more than any other industry, mail order is perfectly positioned to take advantage of today's consumer preferences and the business procedures and strategies that will become more and more common as we move into the 21st Century. No, it's not a sure thing. Nothing is in the world of business. But there's every reason to believe that with intelligent and careful planning you can start and grow a successful mail-order business.

This book has been written to show you the nuts and bolts of doing just that. It discusses where mail order has been, and more importantly, where it's going and why it's such a promising business for entrepreneurs from all walks of life. You'll encounter case histories of both successes and failures as well as advice from many who have succeeded in a variety of mail-order ventures.

The book has also been written to show you how, with an investment of $10,000 or less, you can get started in the mail-order business. Obviously, you're not going to have Spiegel and L. L. Bean shaking in their boots, at least not at first. But with the technology that's available, and with careful control of your advertising, your order processing, and your inventory, you can indeed start a viable mail-order business that can be fun—and more importantly, profitable—right out of the gate.

As we move through the chapters, we'll discuss the step-by-step processes you'll need to go through to start your business.

- Chapter 2 will look at the mail-order industry, its history, how it's growing and changing, and the reasons it's such a promising industry for the 21st Century.
- Chapter 3 will help you do a quick self-analysis to see if you've got the right personality for your entrepreneurial endeavor.
- Chapter 4 will look at how many mail-order businesses can be started for less than $10,000, including what I call the 12 Rules for Doing It Cheaply.
- Chapter 5 will discuss financing needs and where you can look for seed money for your new venture.
- Chapter 6 will look at what you can sell, the factors that

make certain products more attractive than others, and how to evaluate a product's earning potential.

- Chapter 7 will discuss test marketing, to determine whether or not your chosen product or products will really fly with your customers.

- Chapter 8 will show you what you need to do to set up your business, from selecting the right location to obtaining the proper licenses and permits.

- Chapter 9 will help you prepare one of the most important tools needed to run any business—the business plan.

- Chapter 10 will show you how to reach your customers through advertising, direct mail, and many other media.

- Chapter 11 will examine the most important trend in business in decades—doing business on the Internet. It's the perfect medium for mail order and just might be critical to your success.

- Chapter 12 looks at the nuts and bolts of the business—processing orders and shipping merchandise. It also discusses postal regulations and some of the Federal Trade Commission rules governing mail order.

- Chapter 13 examines the day-to-day operation of your business and what you'll need to do to remain happy and profitable over the long haul.

FOR MORE INFORMATION

Throughout this book, I'll be suggesting other sources of information on starting a mail-order business. No book on this topic would be complete without mentioning Julian L. Simon's *How to Start and Operate a Mail Order Business* (McGraw-Hill, Inc.). Now in its fifth edition, Simon's book is a classic that for more than twenty years has helped entrepreneurs get into the mail-order business. It's available at most large bookstores and libraries.

2

NOTHING BUT GROWTH AHEAD

Today, retail mail order grosses $123 billion a year. If current projections are accurate, next year that figure will approach $140 billion. The year after that, more than $150 billion. Is $200 billion a year far off? Certainly not. Could it reach $300 billion? Sure. In fact, it's probably closer than you think.

It's hard to believe that an industry of this size can be considered "untapped," but that's exactly what many business experts—including me—feel about mail order. Why do we feel this way? Let's take a look.

MAIL ORDER IS CONVENIENT

Mail order is popular and will become even more popular for a very simple reason—it's convenient. Not everyone subscribes to the "shop 'til you drop" credo. Personally, the very thought of a shopping trip fills me with such overwhelming dread and fatigue that I can barely stagger out to the car. I'm more of a "let your fingers do the walking" kind of guy.

That's why I love mail order. And if you're like millions of other Americans, you feel the same way. Shopping simply isn't much fun for a lot of people. For them, it's just another annoying task, like putting the snow tires on the car or cleaning out the gutters. They hate the crowds, the noise, the traffic, and the endless visual clutter. So the ability to purchase things over the phone, through the mail, or by computer is a blessing. It

15

means they can avoid a trip downtown or to the dreaded mall, leaving them time to do more of the things they enjoy.

Let's say fall is approaching and you and your spouse decide you've been frugal long enough. It's time to treat yourselves to some new clothes. No problem. You pour some coffee, sit down on the couch with a pile of catalogs, and have fun critiquing each other's selections.

You begin by pouring through catalogs from J. Crew, Eddie Bauer, L. L. Bean, and many other companies that offer all sorts of clothing for both sexes. Then you pick up some men's specialty catalogs like Brooks Brothers and Jos. A. Bank, which sell everything from socks and underwear to tuxedos and cashmere topcoats. Women's specialty shops like Talbot's, Ann Taylor, and Carroll Reed offer gorgeous clothing for women, both casual and formal. You might even give Victoria's Secret a quick look. The catalogs are handsomely produced with quality four-color photographs and informative written descriptions of each item.

Then the kids get wind of what's going on and they start lobbying for a few things. It starts with new clothes but soon escalates into other areas of serious deprivation. Your multi-sport athlete claims to need a new pair of soccer shoes, ski gloves, and the latest high-tech graphite composite hockey stick. He somehow manages to magically produce catalogs that carry these items.

Your resident musicologist demands equal attention and is soon throwing catalogs in front of you listing the dozens of compact discs needed to augment an already absurdly large collection. Then your budding Picasso begins whining about the special tubes of French oil paints and handmade sable brushes that are absolutely critical if anything worthwhile is going to be produced. And, amazingly, Picasso also happens to have the catalogs from which these wonderful things can be obtained.

Finally, when everyone has made their choices, you dust off your credit card and pick up the phone. Everything the family wants can be purchased by merely calling a few toll-free numbers and spending a couple of minutes on the phone with some pleasant customer service representatives. You're buying from names you trust, whose products are durable and of high quality. You feel comfortable spending your money with these companies even though you won't get your first real look at the items you've bought until they show up on your doorstep.

SHOPPING IS INCONVENIENT

As you've already learned, I hate to shop. And I think a lot of other people feel the same way. Let's look at some of the hassles of contemporary shopping and how mail order helps us avoid them.

The Service is Lousy

There was a time when being a retail salesperson was a proud occupation for many people. They were knowledgeable about their merchandise, cared about their customers, and took pride in providing the best service. They worked for commission and made nice incomes after establishing a regular clientele.

Today, the professional salesperson is a dying breed. With their eyes fixed on the bottom line, many retailers rely upon salespeople who are willing to work part-time and for little more than minimum wage. They're usually students, people augmenting their incomes from other jobs, or retirees who are either doing it to keep busy or because they need to supplement their social security. They're woefully undertrained, don't know the merchandise, and, although pleasant, they're usually no help at all.

Mail-order catalogs avoid all this. They provide good service because they include detailed descriptions of the merchandise, clearly state the shipping and return policies, and include a toll-free number to call if you have any unanswered questions. And when you call it, you get someone who knows what they're talking about.

The Hours are Limited

Finding the time to shop can be difficult, particularly for single parents, dual-income families, and people who travel a lot for their jobs. Since retail stores have limited hours, it's not always easy for people to get to them. Mail-order companies, on the other hand, are usually open at least six days a week, twelve or more hours a day. Some of the biggest, such as L. L. Bean, have service representatives on duty twenty-four hours a day, seven days a week. Many also have twenty-four-hour fax lines. No matter how busy someone is, he can always find a few minutes to get on the phone and place an order.

GETTING THERE'S A DRAG

Shopping usually means driving. For some people it means driving fairly long distances. In cities it means fighting terrible traffic. Wherever you are, it means paying for the gasoline, the wear and tear on your car, and a certain amount of time lost from your day. Who needs it?

Buying by mail order means buying from the comfort of your own home, saving time, and avoiding the annoyances of driving.

RETURNING MERCHANDISE MEANS MAKING THE TRIP ALL OVER AGAIN

If you decide you don't like what you bought or find something wrong with it, you have to repeat your trip. If your purchase is from a mail-order company, all you have to do is stick it back in the mailbox. And many companies will accept returned merchandise that is delivered to them COD.

THE SELECTIONS ARE CONFUSING

Have you bought stereo equipment lately? Or a television, power tools, or even *running shoes?* There's simply too much to pick from. There are dozens of choices, each with special features you may or may not want or need. And as we learned earlier, the chances of finding a salesperson who can sort it all out for you are virtually nil.

Mail-order companies, on the other hand, provide complete descriptions of their merchandise to help you wade through the confusion. In the case of technically complex merchandise like stereo equipment, the best companies will even include special sections in their catalogs that educate consumers on terminology and help them determine their needs.

Stores Don't Always Have What They Advertise

Recently, we were in the market for a new VCR. A major retailer in the mall in my town was having a sale on electronic equipment and had a few models that interested me. I drove up to the mall, found a VCR I liked, and spent a few minutes trying to discuss its merits with a very earnest young man who clearly had no idea what he was talking about.

After going through the owner's manual myself, I decided it would meet my needs and told him I would buy it. He disappeared for a few minutes and then returned, sheepishly explaining that they were out of stock and wouldn't be getting any more in because the model had been discontinued.

Well, knowing my love for shopping, you can imagine how happy I was. I had just wasted most of my evening! I stormed out, went home, and dug out the catalog of a large, nationally known electronics company. I called their 800 number and a very competent service rep took my order, checked their inventory to make sure they had the same model in stock, and sent it on its way. And it was fifteen bucks cheaper than the one at the store!

PEOPLE HAVE LESS TIME

Feel a bit stressed sometimes? You're not alone. The pace of modern life seems to be accelerating faster than ever before. There just doesn't seem to be enough time to get everything done. As a result, particularly for today's dual-income, pressed-for-time families, time has become a prized commodity.

That's another reason for mail order's popularity. It saves us lots and lots of time. Let's say you've promised your kids a trip to a ball game on Saturday afternoon. But you also need to buy Uncle Ed a birthday gift. You realize you won't have time to get something during the week on the way home from work; you've got to get to a meeting one night and pick the kids up from various lessons and sports practices on others. Saturday morning is out because you need to mow the lawn. And there's no way you're going to miss the football games on Sunday.

The solution? Flip through a few catalogs, spend a few minutes on the phone, and, boom, Uncle Ed's present is on its way. All you have to do is remember what it was you got him when he calls to thank you.

AMERICA'S DEMOGRAPHICS ARE CHANGING

Demographics are a critical consideration for any business, and mail order is no exception. Fortunately for the industry, demographic trends in the United States point to nothing but growth and profits.

THE TWO-INCOME FAMILY IS HERE TO STAY

The mail-order industry has been experiencing steady growth since the early eighties. In the beginning of that decade, only around 20 percent of adults made purchases via mail order. By the end of the decade, more than 50 percent were using mail order.

Not coincidentally, the eighties were characterized by unprecedented numbers of women entering the workforce. Soon, the two-income family became the rule rather than the exception, and suddenly there were all these families with a lot of income but very little time. Is it any surprise mail order became popular with them?

THE BABY BOOMERS ARE AGING

A significant number of these people, if not the majority of them, were baby boomers, born between 1945 and 1955. Now, as we approach the end of the century, the boomers are hitting middle age and reaching the upper levels of their earning power; more than 30 percent of American households have a net worth of at least $100,000.

They're an interesting group. They're well educated and worldly. They have a fair amount of discretionary income and like to spend money on themselves. They dote on their children and value education. They're also health conscious and environmentally aware.

But most importantly, they're very, very busy. Between their jobs and their leisure time activities, they've little time for shopping. They'd rather enjoy sports or travel or participating in their kids' activities. Given their hectic lifestyles, sometimes they just like to lie around and do nothing. When they need to shop, they open a catalog.

There's a Second Wave Behind the Boomers

The aging of the baby boom generation doesn't mean there won't be enough children and adolescents for marketers to reach. Since 1985, thanks to the efforts of the youngest of the baby boomers, the number of children born each year has increased by 100,000 a year. In 1990, the birth rate was higher than in 1950. The U.S. Census Bureau estimates that by 2010, the number of minors in the country will have grown around 10 percent.

All this means the youth market will remain strong. And since, as we've already learned, their parents both work, there will be plenty of opportunity for mail-order businesses to meet their needs.

Single-Parent Households Have Increased

One of the unfortunate statistics in modern America is that roughly half of all marriages end in divorce. Because of this, the number of households with just one parent has risen dramatically. These single parents are wearing all the hats traditionally shared by two people in a marriage—breadwinner, chauffeur, cook, cleaner, launderer, gardener. Think they have much time to run out to the mall? When you have all these other tasks hanging over your head, the ability to shop from home becomes pretty darn attractive.

OUR ELDERLY POPULATION IS ABOUT TO EXPLODE

The United States is about to enter the gerontological age. If that brings dinosaurs to mind, it should. Never in our history have we had as many people over the age of 65 as we do now. Our over-50 population will increase 50 percent in the next 20 years, from 65 million to 97 million. And the number of very old, those over 85, is also soon going to reach an all-time high.

What do these figures mean for the mail-order industry? First of all, this older generation—or the "Ikes," as they're sometimes known—will go down as the wealthiest in the history of our nation. They've done well, and they want to live out their golden years in style. So mail-order businesses that cater to their needs and interests should prosper.

THE CULTURAL TEXTURE OF AMERICA IS CHANGING

The United States is increasingly a patchwork quilt of different cultures. As more and more immigrants are assimilated into our society, they create markets for new products and services and increased opportunities for mail-order businesses.

One of the best examples is the nation's Hispanic population. With an estimated $175 billion in purchasing power, America's 24 million Hispanics are the second-fastest growing population group in the country and the most lucrative ethnic market. Manufacturers in all sorts of industries are developing new products to cater to Hispanic tastes. Advertising expenditures in the Hispanic market are approaching $1 billion a year. And there's nothing but growth ahead. Conservative estimates predict that by the year 2015, there will be 40 million Hispanics in the United States. By the year 2030, they may represent as much as $500 billion in purchasing power.

IT'S NOT REALLY "MAIL" ORDER ANYMORE

The evolution of the mail-order industry has been inextricably tied to the development of communication in this country. But today, although the name will probably never change, "mail" order is really no longer an accurate description of what has become a relatively sophisticated industry.

THE EARLY DAYS OF MAIL ORDER

Mail order got its name because originally that's exactly what it was. People placed orders through the mail, and eventually their package would arrive through the mail. Back in the early days of the industry, the arrival of that package was no doubt one of the most eagerly awaited moments of the week.

This was the latter half of the nineteenth century, when the only way people in America's rural corners could regularly communicate with one another and with their city cousins was through the mail. The sprawl and limited mobility of the population also presented a challenge to merchandisers. In the cities, precursors to today's department stores were beginning to flourish. They were big stores with a wide variety of merchandise that attracted many, many customers. Although any number of these stores were quite prosperous, their customer base was limited to those people who could reach their stores by foot or via horseback or horse-drawn carriage.

Like all good businesspeople, these merchandisers knew they were missing a significant segment of the population, but they didn't know what to do about it. The solution soon came to them: sell their goods through the mail.

One of the first big mail-order companies was Sears & Roebuck. Founded in 1886 in Chicago, a strategic location from which to reach the rest of the country, they sold just about everything. You could even purchase a *house* from them. It wasn't long before the Sears & Roebuck catalog was a staple in homes throughout rural America. And when a new one arrived, the old one was frequently put to use out in the family privy.

Other companies soon followed, and for the next seventy or eighty years, the mail-order industry remained virtually unchanged. Customers would fill out an order form, stick it an envelope with a check or a money order, and then wait weeks or even months for their merchandise to arrive.

Sometimes their purchases didn't show up at all. The industry in its early days was plagued by fly-by-night operators who would run an ad, collect the money, and then fail to deliver the merchandise. Another problem was the abundance of shoddy merchandise that was peddled by mail-order companies. Once customers received their orders, they more often than not were stuck, regardless of whether or not they were happy with the quality of their purchases.

Not surprisingly, much of the public tended to regard mail order with a raised eyebrow. But that gradually changed. Over the years, postal regulators cracked down on mail-order crooks, and regulations were enacted to provide stiff penalties for mail fraud. Other legislation was created to make mail-order companies more considerate of the rights of the consumer. The quality of merchandise became more consistent, and it became easier to return merchandise that was unsatisfactory. (We'll look at the rules and regulations governing mail order in chapter 12.)

Despite these efforts, however, mail order still had one major drawback—the amount of time it took to receive merchandise. Virtually all business was still conducted via the mail and with checks. First, your order had to get to its destination and be processed. Then the company had to wait until your check cleared before it would ship your merchandise. Then you had to wait for your package to wind its way through the circuitous maze of the United States Postal Service.

THE IMPACT OF THE CREDIT CARD

During the sixties and seventies, mail order suddenly began to get easier, and for one simple reason—the credit card. Customers could call a mail-order company on its toll-free 800 number, place their order, and give the company a credit card number, to which the company could bill the purchase. The bank providing the card would pay the mail-order company and assume the task of collecting the money from the consumer. The order could be filled almost immediately and sent on its way. All by itself, that little piece of plastic removed a huge chunk of time from the process. All the consumer had to do was place an order and hope the USPS could find his house.

Then even that became less of a problem. The sixties and seventies also saw the growing popularity of package delivery services that went nose to nose against the post office. United Parcel Service, Federal Express, and many other companies offered swift delivery at reasonable prices. Their success made the USPS take notice, and its package delivery service began to improve as well.

Today, around 80 percent of American adults have at least one credit card. Some people have five or six or more. There are currently nearly 900 million credit cards in the United States with almost $3 trillion in buying power. Annual credit card spending is approaching $450 billion a year, and it's still growing. Some cards are issued by major retailers like Sears or J. C. Penney. Others are bank cards like VISA and MasterCard. Still others are from gasoline companies or third-party cards like American Express, Diner's Club, and Discover.

Mail Order Today

Even by the eighties, as mail order really came into its own, the term "mail" order was no longer descriptive of the way the industry worked. Many customers today place their orders over the phone or by fax, using the all-powerful credit card to pay for their purchases.

While the credit card will continue to be the vehicle that makes mail order quick and easy, procedures for ordering merchandise will continue to evolve, largely due to the growing popularity of personal computers and use of the Internet to conduct business. As we'll see in chapter 11, the electronic storefront is already a reality, and people who have access to the Internet are furiously buying and selling goods and services in cyberspace. And it's only the beginning.

In the meantime, thousands of mail-order businesses are thriving and looking toward an even better future. Many retailers with established "storefront" locations are venturing into mail order. Some of them may find that their mail-order volume will eventually surpass their store volume.

Some competing mail-order companies are actually owned by the same parent company and share the same customer service locations. A friend of mine found this out quite by accident one evening when she was ordering some clothing from different catalogs. She told me about it the next day.

"I called the first company and got this pleasant guy with a real nice, laid-back southern accent," she recalled. "They had to back-order some of the stuff and the whole thing got fairly complicated, but he was really nice through it all. It got fairly chatty, and the whole exchange was very pleasant.

"Then I hung up and called the next company and the same guy answered. I thought I had redialed the first number and got sort of flustered and began stammering an apology. But he recognized my voice and started laughing.

" 'Well, now you know our little secret,' he said."

WHAT SELLS?

Clothing, sporting goods, and compact discs are just the tip of the mail-order iceberg that has been growing like crazy in the waters of American retailing over the last fifteen years. You can also buy jewelry, furniture, kitchenware, cosmetics, electronic equipment, plants, food, vitamins, and thousands of other items. If there's a market for it, and it can be delivered via the United States Postal Service, United Parcel Service, Federal Express, or any of the other package delivery services, chances are it's being sold by mail order.

A look around the industry will show you just how diverse the offerings are. Obviously, there are hundreds of companies selling the usual items like clothing and jewelry and books. But there are also many companies specializing in things that might be considered a bit more esoteric.

- For science teachers and others fascinated by the wonders of the human skeleton, Ambiomed International in Lake

Park, Florida, offers a nice selection of "plastic and natural bone teaching aids."

- Fans of the early days of the movie industry will love Grapevine Video in Phoenix. Their 32-page catalog has nothing but videos of silent screen classics.

- If you're into the proud history of bowling, Formula Impressions in St. Louis carries an extensive collection of old bowling shirts. They also do embroidery and custom work.

- A lot of food companies specialize in just one or two regional items. For instance, Piggie Park Enterprises in West Columbia, South Carolina, sells nothing but barbecue sauce. The Ontario Produce Co. in Ontario, Oregon, sells nothing but onions.

- You can even buy bottled water through the mail. The Water of the Month Club offers a nice selection of domestic and imported bottled waters. Based in Edison, New Jersey (where bottled water is probably an excellent idea), the company has been in business since 1990 and accepts VISA, MasterCard, and American Express.

- Many of my favorite companies fall into the novelty gifts category. It's amazing what you can buy. Graceland Gifts in Memphis sells Elvis memorabilia. The National Football League, the TV show *Cheers,* and Warner Brothers Studios all have catalogs. Lefthanded Solutions in Port Jefferson Station, New York, sells nothing but gifts for lefties. For Counsel in West Linn, Oregon, sells nothing but gifts for *lawyers.* But my favorite is Gifts Anon in Phoenix, which sells—you guessed it—gifts for people in twelve-step recovery programs.

The lesson to be learned from this is that anything—and I mean *anything*—can be sold through mail order. Keep this in mind later on when we discuss what you should sell. In the meantime, here are some of the product areas that racked up the biggest sales volumes in 1993.

FINANCIAL SERVICES—$19.7 BILLION

Insurance and other financial services have proven to mesh quite well with mail order and direct marketing strategies. Although it's highly unlikely you'll be involved in this type of business as a start-up mail-order concern, it serves to illustrate the wide range of things that can be sold, and that "tangible" products aren't the only thing that can be sold.

HOUSEWARES, GIFTS, AND GENERAL MERCHANDISE— $17.4 BILLION

There's a lot of money to be made furnishing America's homes and supplying its gift needs. This product area has always been a cornerstone of the industry and will continue to perform well in the future.

CLOTHING—$16.5 BILLION

No mystery here. Everybody needs clothes, and the average consumer probably spends more on clothing than on any other item each year. The most innovative (and profitable) companies in recent years have identified their target markets and gone after them with finely tuned product lines. Clothing has been and will always be a mail-order staple.

MAGAZINES—$8 BILLION

Magazine subscription sales are a huge mail-order business, although, again, it's an unlikely candidate for most people starting up a new business.

SPORTING GOODS—$6.5 BILLION

Sports and fitness are boom industries in the United States, and companies specializing in mail-order sporting goods are enjoying every minute of it. Golf, basketball, skiing, aerobics, racquet sports, biking, camping, hunting and fishing, running, rock climbing, boating—people today are involved in more sports than ever before. And they're willing to pay for quality, high-priced equipment. For example, a good set of golf clubs—including irons, woods, and a putter—can easily cost $800 to $1,000. Throw in the shoes, a bag, a dozen golf balls, and the proper attire designed to make you look like the pros, and you've added another $300 to $400. This should be a growth area for quite some time and is ripe for the clever marketer with attractive products.

ELECTRONICS—$5.9 BILLION

This segment of the industry has been strong for the past fifteen years and will continue to grow. Televisions and audio equipment will always be popular items, the electronic game industry continues to churn out new products, and there are still many, many homes in this country without computers. Another area to watch is the ongoing evolution of the Internet. Its potential impact on both business and leisure activities is just beginning to be realized, and it will no doubt spawn all sorts of electronic gadgets.

COLLECTIBLES—$2.7 BILLION

Coins, stamps, baseball cards, military memorabilia, miniatures, and other collectibles have long been popular mail-order products. Also popular are limited edition commemorative plates and other items you'll see advertised in the magazine supplement of your Sunday newspaper. Collectibles have historically been a strong segment of the industry, and, although sales of more expensive items can be affected during times of recession, should continue to experience above-average growth.

BOOKS—$2.4 BILLION

Books have long been a popular mail-order item, but sales have proven vulnerable to economic fluctuations and rising paper costs. Regardless of the economy, a carefully managed mail-order book business can perform admirably.

CRAFTS—$1.6 BILLION

Although crafts are still a significant part of the industry, they're not as popular as they were ten or fifteen years ago. The main reason for this is the large number of women who entered the workforce during the eighties. In addition, kids are no longer as interested in crafts as they once were. Now they spend their time with video games and other forms of electronic entertainment. This is not to say that crafts are dead. They'll certainly continue to be popular, particularly as baby boomers begin to retire and take up pottery, painting, and other hobbies. But mail-order crafts businesses must pay extra-close attention to their products and their market.

COMPACT DISCS AND TAPES—$1.6 BILLION

The industry has a number of music "clubs" that sell everything from classical and opera to rap and hip-hop. There are also dozens of smaller companies specializing in hard-to-find music or in certain types of music. My own gut feeling is that a mail-order business specializing in classic vinyl LPs would do well; there's a growing subculture of audiophiles who are clamoring for the "warmer" sound they claim old-fashioned vinyl produces. Recorded music in all its forms is certainly a market that's here for the long term. But since it's tied somewhat to the availability of discretionary income, it can have peaks and valleys. (In chapter 11, we'll meet one compact disc retailer who has set up shop on the Internet.)

THE IMPORTANCE OF MAILING LISTS

If you have a mailbox, I don't have to do much explaining about the use of catalogs by mail-order companies. I'm sure you receive half a dozen or more each week. They're by far the most efficient vehicle anyone has found for reaching the customer. They're also the most widely used. Just ask the poor guy who delivers your mail.

To make sure their catalogs (or advertisements or flyers) reach the right customers, mail-order companies maintain carefully structured mailing lists. They include past customers as well as people who haven't done business with them before. The demographic accuracy of these lists is absolutely critical. If companies are sending catalogs to people who have no interest in the sort of thing they sell, or who can't afford the merchandise, they might as well burn them.

Let's look at how mail-order companies have targeted my family to see how mailing lists work.

Our Lives as Demographic Targets

My family is probably about as demographically average as you could ask for. My wife and I both work, we have two kids and two dogs, we own a house and a car, and we lease a second car. We have just about every appliance on the market (except a microwave oven, which amazes our friends), and we have the usual complement of electronic gizmos. We're also in an income bracket that makes us attractive to merchandisers. A quick look at the catalogs that arrive at our home will show you how eager they are to have us as customers.

During a two-month period in 1995, the following companies and institutions sent us catalogs or other promotional materials. Most sent several catalogs. Some sent something every week.

In no particular order, the companies were: L. L. Bean, Crabtree & Evelyn, Norm Thompson, Victoria's Secret, J. Crew, MacWarehouse, Dartek Computer Supply, Crate & Barrel, Pottery Barn, Edmund Scientific, Eddie Bauer, Horchow Home Collection, Jackson & Perkins Roses and Gardens, Sears, The Sharper Image, Fingerhut, California Best, Tweed's, Crutchfield's, Omaha Steaks International, Sugar Hill, The Metropolitan Museum of Art, Williams-Sonoma, Sundance, Talbot's, Plow & Hearth, Anticipations, Edwin Watts Golf Shops, Campmor, WinterSilks, Lillian Vernon, Land's End, Ikea, Hammacher Schlemmer, Flax Art & Design, Ocean Hockey Supply, Pearl Paint Co., American Family Publishers, The Mac Zone, Ross-Simons of Warwick, and Breck's Dutch Bulbs (pause for breath).

We also heard from the Book-of-the-Month Club, Domestications, Miller's Riding Supply, The Boston Museum of Fine Arts, Tiffany & Co., Columbia House Records and Tapes, The Body Shop, Time-Life Books, Smith & Hawken, The Art Institute of Chicago, The Company Store, Brooks Brothers, Banana

Republic, The Wine Enthusiast, J. Peterman, Brownstone Studio, Golfsmith, Chadwick's of Boston, Neiman-Marcus, Winterthur Museum and Gardens, Spiegel, J. C. Penney, The Nature Company, F. A. O. Schwartz, MacConnection, Paragon, The Bombay Company, Clifford & Wills, Burpee Seed Co., Charles Keith Ltd., Coach Leatherware, Hickory Farms, The Swiss Colony, Wolferman's, Gardener's Eden, Kemp's Hockey Supply, and (listed last because I like their name so much) Klutz Enterprises.

THEY KNOW WE'RE OUT THERE, AND THEY'D LOVE TO HEAR FROM US

The amazing thing is that we've probably purchased goods from fewer than half of these companies. So why do we hear from the rest? It's simple. First of all, as I said before, we fit a certain demographic profile. Second, because we've purchased goods from certain companies, others that are in the same business are anxious to find out who we are and where we live so they can sell us stuff, too.

How do the companies we've never dealt with get our names and address? That's also quite simple. They either rent mailing lists from other mail-order companies or trade lists with other companies. They also rent the mailing lists of certain special interest magazines.

For example, I'm sure the reason I receive catalogs from Flax Art & Design and Pearl Paint Co. is the fact that I subscribe to *Art in America.* The companies figure that if I subscribe to the magazine, there's a good chance I'm an artist and therefore a potential customer. Keep all this in mind. We'll discuss mailing lists again when we look at marketing strategies in chapter 10.

WHY MAILING LISTS WORK

Actually, the catalogs received by a household usually paint a very good picture of the people who receive them, so it shouldn't be surprising that companies seek out one another's mailing lists.

For example, my family has been pretty accurately targeted. If you look at the catalogs we receive, you'll get a good idea of the way we dress (Eddie Bauer, J. Crew, L. L. Bean, Tweed's, Banana Republic), what our interests are (Edwin Watts and Golfsmith, Campmor, Columbia House, Breck's Dutch Bulbs and Gardener's Eden, Ocean Hockey Supply, Book-of-the-Month Club, Miller's Riding Supply, Flax Art & Design), and what the inside of our house looks like (Ikea, Pottery Barn, Crate & Barrel, Williams-Sonoma).

You'll also learn what kind of computers we own (MacConnection and MacWarehouse), that we like to buy a lot of our gifts from catalogs (The Company Store, Ross-Simons, The Nature Company, Boston Museum of Fine Arts), and that we probably have at least one adolescent in the house (Klutz Enterprises).

As you can see, mailing lists work. Establishing an accurate mailing list will be one of the most important tasks you'll face in setting up your business.

WHAT'S NEXT?

I hope by now you'll agree with me that mail order is an industry with nothing but growth ahead. It meshes well with our lifestyles, it provides quality merchandise and excellent service, and it avoids a lot of the unpleasant hassles associated with shopping. It offers wonderful opportunities for both the novice entrepreneur and the seasoned businessperson.

There is one "but" to all this, however, and it's a big one. Not everyone is right for business ownership, and those who aren't cut out for it rarely make it. So before you begin planning your mail-order business you'll need to take a hard look at yourself. You'll need to examine your own unique blend of skills, motives, and traits to see if going into business is right for you. That's the subject of chapter 3.

⟨≫⟩·3·⟨≪⟩

ARE YOU READY TO RUN YOUR OWN BUSINESS?

Starting a business is exciting and nerve-wracking. It will be one of the biggest investments you'll make during your lifetime. Not just financially, but emotionally as well. Doing it right will mean taking on a lot of responsibilities and making a lot of sacrifices. It will also mean working harder than you ever have before.

For these reasons, business ownership is not for everyone. If you don't have the right skills, personality, and commitment to operate a business, you'll be in trouble before you make your first sale. So before you begin planning your mail-order business, you need to take a hard look at yourself, your family, and your finances, and give honest answers to some very important questions.

AN ENTREPRENEURIAL SELF-ANALYSIS

The following questions will help you weigh your personal characteristics and beliefs against the realities of business ownership. Don't worry if you find that a few of the questions reveal doubts or weaknesses. Nobody's a perfect match for any profession. But if you find many of the questions troubling, you may want to rethink your decision to go into business.

ARE YOU WILLING TO ACCEPT THE RESPONSIBILITIES OF OPERATING YOUR OWN BUSINESS?

Forget the tidy little set of responsibilities that came with a position in corporate life. When you run a business, you're in

34

charge of everything—from opening the doors in the morning to cleaning up at night. Then when you go home, you worry.

The hours are long, there's a high degree of stress, and there's always too much to do and not enough time to do it. You'll have to deal with your customers and your employees. You'll be responsible for the finances of the business and dealing with taxes. And you'll need to fill out a lot of forms and sign a lot of checks.

Make sure you understand what you're getting into. As a business owner, you'll have more responsibilities than you've ever had before, no matter what your previous jobs have been. If you understand this simple fact, you'll be ready to take your responsibilities on.

ARE YOU COMFORTABLE MAKING HARD DECISIONS?

Before he retired, my father ran a small manufacturing company that employed about forty people. He always said that the biggest pressure of the job was knowing that his decisions determined whether or not these people were able to feed their families.

As the owner of a business, you'll also have to make many decisions that affect the business, your livelihood, and that of your employees. Many times they'll be tough to make, including the decision to lay people off if your business falls on hard times. It will require decisiveness, mental toughness, and resolve. If you have trouble when faced with tough choices, this could be a problem area.

DO YOU THINK OWNING YOUR OWN BUSINESS IS THE ROAD TO EASY MONEY?

Think again. Many people actually end up sacrificing income to open their businesses, at least at first. That's the price they're willing to pay for independence.

If you're thinking of giving up a promising career and a lucrative income to start your business, be realistic about what your financial needs are and whether or not the business will meet those needs. Remember, you're building a business, and it may take you a number of years to get to the income level you want or need. On the other hand, you may decide that you're willing to sacrifice some money for the reward of being your own boss. Many people have found it to be worth every penny.

Consider Steve Larson of Cherry Hill, New Jersey. By most measures of success, he had it made. He was almost twenty years into a successful career with a large insurance firm. He enjoyed a nice salary with excellent benefits and a generous retirement plan. The company was doing well, and there was every opportunity for him to continue up the corporate ladder.

But Steve was bored to tears. He was sick of his rush hour commute across the Delaware River into Philadelphia every day. He was tired of meetings and memos and having to tailor his personality to fit into the corporate culture. It had gotten to the point that some days he could barely make himself go into the office. Finally, he decided to start a business.

That was five years ago. Today Steve is the owner of a thriving mail-order business specializing in software for business office systems. His company is located in a business park ten minutes from his home. He has two full-time employees and two part-timers. And he's having the time of his life.

He started small, running the business out of his basement and devoting evenings and weekends to getting it up and running. After two years, he was generating enough sales volume to make the big move—he quit his job.

"It was the happiest day of my life," he recalls. "I was scared to death, but I knew I was making the right decision. There were big financial sacrifices at first. I started out earning less than half of what I'd made in my old job. But it's gotten better each year, and if business keeps increasing I should be back where I was in another year or two."

Just realize that success in business, like success in anything else, is earned. Granted, if you follow the advice outlined in this book, you'll be off to a good start. And yes, you can make money, sometimes a lot of money. But the critical ingredient is you. You're not going to make money without a lot of sacrifice, dedication, and plain hard work.

ARE YOU STARTING A BUSINESS OUT OF DESPERATION?

This is a very real concern, particularly in light of the huge number of experienced businessmen and businesswomen who have been cast adrift in the job market through corporate downsizing in recent years. If you're one of these people and are thinking about starting a business because you think it's your only option, be very careful. Yes, it can be the answer to your future security, but only if you're willing to make the necessary commitments and sacrifices. The world of business ownership is vastly different from the corporate world. Make sure you recognize the differences before you make the move.

ARE YOU WELL-ORGANIZED?

The day-to-day operation of your business is going to require you to assume many responsibilities. Let's consider an average day. You may need to do the payroll, talk to suppliers, pay a few bills, work on a new advertising pamphlet, and prepare some tax forms. At the same time you'll be filling orders and making sure they get sent out on time. Then there's always the unexpected—your computer bombs or the air-conditioning conks out.

As a business owner, you'll need to keep many balls in the air at one time. Your ability to juggle all these responsibilities will directly affect your success. If you're well organized, you'll have a list of the things you need to do, and you'll methodically go through it during the course of the day. If you're interrupted, you'll pick up where you left off after you've dealt with the problem. If you're still not through at the end of the day, you'll sit there and work until you've finished. Procrastinators do not do well in business. If you get behind, you're sunk.

ARE YOU CREATIVE?

It's an asset to any business. No matter how great your product, you're not going to be the only one selling it. Marketing and advertising are critical to getting customers' attention and encouraging them to buy. If you have a creative streak—whether it be copywriting, graphic design, or even an offbeat sense of humor—it will be an invaluable asset to your business.

This is doubly true in mail order. Since your customers can't see the items they're purchasing "in the flesh," so to speak, they need to be enticed by the visual presentation and written description in your promotional materials. One of the best examples of this is probably the J. Peterman Co. clothing catalog, which uses attractive, loosely rendered gouache illustrations of its merchandise combined with extremely clever ad copy. They also use an odd size (5¼ by 10½ inches) for their catalog, which helps make it stand out from the others that arrive in the mail. For my money, a lot of their stuff is overpriced and kind of silly. But something in that catalog is pushing someone's buttons. The company is not even ten years old, and it is already grossing more than $60 million in sales each year.

ARE YOU FLEXIBLE?

In business, if an idea or plan doesn't work, you can't let yourself waste time, energy, and emotion bemoaning its failure. You need to quickly come up with an alternative solution. Flexibility and adaptability are the key. You'll need to stay focused to achieve your goal, but you may need to try several different paths to get there.

In mail order, for example, one marketing approach may work for a while and then stall. At that point you'll need to come up with something new. Remember, every business plan and every business can benefit from a fresh look every once in a while, even when things seem to be going along just fine.

ARE YOU GOAL ORIENTED?

This trait is obviously helpful in all parts of life, but it's particularly helpful in business. As a business owner, your goals will be defined in very simple, concrete terms—gross sales and net profit.

A good businessperson approaches each year with new goals and uses them as motivating forces throughout the year. Let's say gross sales for your first year of operation were $150,000 and your net profit was $40,000. For the following year, you might set as your goal a 20 percent increase, or $180,000 and $48,000. Achieving or surpassing those figures will drive you day after day.

Goal-oriented people also plan for the future. Eventually, you may want to expand your product selection and your target market. You'll have a long-term plan that includes the timing of your expansion and what every aspect of your business will do to accommodate increased volume.

ARE YOU AN OPTIMIST?

Having the right mental attitude is important for every aspect of life. When you run into hard times, keeping an upbeat attitude and looking for the positive side of things is critical to riding out the storm.

This is particularly true in business. By nature, it's a trip with peaks and valleys. For instance, the hardest time for any business is the first year or two. You may spend months getting things ready to go, carefully selecting the merchandise you'll carry, and getting your advertising strategy together. Then you'll send out your first mailing and wait anxiously for the phone to begin ringing off the hook and your mailbox to be jammed with orders.

But nothing happens. Maybe a few orders trickle in, or you get some phone calls with questions about certain items. This isn't unusual, but even knowing that, you'll still worry. If you're the type of person who gets down when things don't quite go the way you'd like, you might have trouble with the roller coaster ride that any business will take you on. Keeping a positive mental attitude is essential to weathering the bad times and working hard to make the good ones arrive that much sooner.

HAVE YOU HAD EXPERIENCE YOU CAN USE IN RUNNING THE BUSINESS?

If you have, it will make learning the business a lot easier. Experience in sales, accounting, advertising, marketing, personnel management, taxes, or any other business-related responsibility is a definite plus for a potential business owner.

Experience with computers is also important. Few businesses these days operate with old-fashioned ledgers, spreadsheets, and inventory lists. It's all done electronically. When you fill an order, a computer will register the transaction, print a receipt to send with the order, and remove the item or items from your inventory. You'll probably use various software programs to keep track of your bank accounts, your income and expenses, your projected sales, and other information.

The role of computers in small businesses such as mail order will soon expand even further. Using their computers and modems, more and more businesses are connecting to the Internet, specifically the World Wide Web, a graphics intensive application that's rapidly becoming the most popular vehicle for Internet communication. Because it allows users to include photographs, illustrations, and graphics, as well as text, on their electronic pages, the Web is tailor-made for mail-order businesses.

To the uninitiated, computers can be intimidating. But learning how to use them is really quite easy, and the benefits they bring to both our businesses and personal lives is immeasurable. If you're well schooled in their use, it's to your advantage. If you're not, it's time to learn.

DO YOU ENJOY WORKING WITH PEOPLE?

One of the painful realities of being in retail is the fact that the customer is always right. Granted, running a mail-order business distances you from your customers in the sense that there's rarely face-to-face contact. But that doesn't mean you don't owe them the same service and courtesy you would if they were standing right in front of you.

As a mail-order retailer, you'll have the same problems with customers that storefront retailers experience. You'll have complaints about your merchandise, your prices, your service, your policies, and your employees. Believe me, no matter how well you think you have things organized, someone will find fault with them.

This is where tact, patience, and understanding come in. When a customer is unhappy, you must put up with their behavior and try to amend the situation. The last thing your business needs is a bad reputation. If you allow a customer to go away unsatisfied, you can be sure the person will tell all their friends how terrible you are. That, in turn, will keep a lot of potential customers from becoming regular customers.

So there will be times when you'll have to bite the bullet and make amends quickly and courteously when you'd really like to tell the customer to take a hike. Because you're dealing with someone who may be halfway across the country, it may take a personal phone call, an overnight special delivery, or a refund with a handwritten note saying you're sorry the purchase didn't work out but you look forward to helping them in the future. Just make sure you leave the customer happy. (Chapter 13 has some advice on dealing with unhappy customers.)

You'll also have to deal with the people who work for you. As the owner of a business, your behavior will set the standard for your employees' behavior. If you're negative and critical, they'll be negative and critical. But if you're cheerful and upbeat, that will also be reflected in their behavior.

You'll have to be tough at times. Managing people isn't easy. If you're lucky, most of your employees will be pleasant, will work hard, and will contribute positively to the business. But you'll also have a few who will turn out to be unpleasant, lazy, incompetent, or even dishonest. Motivating them will be a challenge. If you can't change their behavior, you have to be able to fire them. (Chapter 13 also has advice on employee relations.)

Are You Comfortable Dealing with Money?

Some people are terribly inept at finances. Others can do it but hate it. Like it or not, financial management is an inescapable fact of business ownership. You'll be dealing with complex monetary issues, from financing the business to handling the day-to-day receipts. You'll be responsible for paying the bills, making the bank deposits, doing the payroll, and sending in withholding taxes and quarterly reports to the IRS and the state. You may be handling substantial amounts of cash, and there are certain risks inherent in that responsibility.

You'll also be making business plans. These are detailed projections of your income and expenses for a given period of time, usually three months, six months, or a year. In some ways, they're quite simple—you want to maximize your income and minimize your expenses. But they take careful planning and budgeting. What are the minimum staffing expenses going to be to operate the business? What will your overhead and utilities be? How much money can you spend on advertising? When are the taxes due? How will you determine the price of your products? What will you charge for shipping and handling?

Any financial experience you may have had will help you with this aspect of your business. And if you like this type of activity, it will be to your advantage. But if you find it burdensome, you'll have to be ready to deal with it.

ARE YOU FINANCIALLY PREPARED TO OPEN A BUSINESS?

Starting any business requires money. The nice thing about mail order is that you can make it about as bare-bones as you care to, particularly if you're starting a small operation that you'll operate in your spare time. Many people have started mail-order businesses for just a few hundred dollars.

But the bigger your dreams, the more money you're going to need. If you're planning a full-time mail-order business with numerous products, the start-up costs will be considerably higher. Then a whole new batch of considerations comes into play. Do you have the financial reserves to support you and your family for a period of time until business picks up? Some business advisers say you should have enough on hand to survive for a year with no income whatsoever. While that may be an unrealistic goal, you do need to consider what happens if the business fails altogether. Do you have the resources to weather such a catastrophe?

Before you begin planning your business, you need to take a careful look at your finances. How much of your available capital are you willing to risk? Are you willing to personally sign for a business loan? What do you have to offer as collateral? How much cash will you have in reserve for emergencies? If you don't have enough to start the business yourself, are you willing to take on a partner or partners? Are you staking your entire financial future on the business?

Undercapitalization is *the* main cause of failure for small businesses in the United States. Yet many people, caught up in the entrepreneurial fever, continue to start businesses on a shoestring, woefully unprepared to deal with the bad times. If you can't start your business with a comfortable financial cushion beneath you, you may be taking a risk you can't afford.

IS YOUR FAMILY READY TO MAKE THE COMMITMENT?

Whether your family is actively involved in the business or not, business ownership is going to have a huge effect on them. If you're the only one involved in its day-to-day operation, the rest of the family isn't going to see you very much. If they're used to having you around on evenings and weekends, this may cause problems.

Your spouse may be unhappy having less time to go out to dinner or the movies. Your absence may also mean he or she is going to have to assume a lot more responsibility at home—chauffeuring the kids here and there, helping with homework, doing the shopping, cooking the meals, cleaning the house, paying the bills, and all the other odds and ends that are part of day-to-day life.

Your kids may have to make some big adjustments, too. You might not be available for Little League games, dance recitals, school plays, and all the other events of childhood.

There may also be some financial adjustments for your family. If you're like most fledgling business owners, you'll be running a tight ship for a few years. Your family will have to realize there might not be money for some of the luxuries they used to take for granted.

It's extremely important to think about potential family problems early in the process. Sit everyone down together and tell them what you're thinking of doing. Make sure they know what it will mean to the family's day-to-day routine and find out how they feel about it. Their support will make your life a lot easier. You're going to have enough stress just handling the business. The last thing you'll need is a family crisis.

The other side of the coin is having your family members working in the business with you. The dynamics of family businesses can be quite volatile, and you'll want to make sure everyone can get along. A major question will be, Who's the boss? Are the lines of authority clearly drawn? Are you and your spouse going to be equals in ownership and operation of the business? If so, are you able to work together cheerfully and consider each other's opinions? If you are, you'll probably have no problem running the company together. But if you can't even agree on what kind of soap to use, you may have trouble.

CAN YOU HANDLE STRESS?

It comes with the territory. Long hours, endless responsibility, dealing with customers, worrying about money—these can take a huge emotional toll. Some people thrive on stress. It actually makes them perform better. They stay calm in a crisis and can react quickly to change. Others fall apart when things get too hectic. Which kind of person are you?

ARE YOU IN GOOD HEALTH?

Running a business can be physically taxing as well. You may have to spend a lot of time on your feet and not get as much sleep as you'd like. You may not have as much time to eat properly or exercise regularly. There may be activities in the business that require a fair amount of physical strength.

Take an inventory of your physical health. Do you have any chronic problems that might prevent you from operating the business efficiently? Remember, when you own the business, you have to be there day after day. A long absence because of a serious illness could spell disaster.

THE ENTREPRENEURIAL POTENTIAL QUIZ

The 25 questions in this quiz are designed to measure competitiveness, self-reliance, patience, emotional stability, flexibility, objectivity, and other important entrepreneurial traits. When you've finished, you can total your score to see how you might fare as a business owner. Give yourself 4 points for each A answer, 3 points for each B answer, 2 points for each C answer, and 1 point for each D answer.

1. I would readily give up the security of working for someone else for the autonomy of running my own business, even if it meant more work and less pay.
   A. strongly agree
   B. moderately agree
   C. moderately disagree
   D. strongly disagree

2. I'm more determined than most people and can do just about anything I set my mind to.
   A. strongly agree
   B. moderately agree
   C. moderately disagree
   D. strongly disagree

3. I have a sharp, analytical mind.
   A. strongly agree
   B. moderately agree
   C. moderately disagree
   D. strongly disagree

4. I've worked long hours for extended periods of time in my previous jobs, and I'd still be willing and able to do so if necessary.
   A. strongly agree
   B. moderately agree
   C. moderately disagree
   D. strongly disagree

5. I've always been driven to be the best in everything I do.
  A. strongly agree
  B. moderately agree
  C. moderately disagree
  D. strongly disagree

6. I can deal with chronic problems and obstacles without getting frustrated or losing my temper.
  A. strongly agree
  B. moderately agree
  C. moderately disagree
  D. strongly disagree

7. I welcome a challenge and hate to feel like I'm wasting my time on routine tasks.
  A. strongly agree
  B. moderately agree
  C. moderately disagree
  D. strongly disagree

8. I value competence over personality, and would rather work with a difficult person who's competent than a person who's very congenial but less competent.
  A. strongly agree
  B. moderately agree
  C. moderately disagree
  D. strongly disagree

9. I'm more likely to organize a group of people and take charge than to follow the lead of others.
  A. strongly agree
  B. moderately agree
  C. moderately disagree
  D. strongly disagree

10. I'm more comfortable making decisions and giving orders than having decisions made for me and taking orders.
A. strongly agree
B. moderately agree
C. moderately disagree
D. strongly disagree

11. I'm efficient and able to stick to a strict timetable in order to complete tasks in a timely way.
A. strongly agree
B. moderately agree
C. moderately disagree
D. strongly disagree

12. I'd value my employees' well-being, but not at the expense of my business.
A. strongly agree
B. moderately agree
C. moderately disagree
D. strongly disagree

13. Given reasonable odds, my efforts usually influence the outcome of an endeavor.
A. strongly agree
B. moderately agree
C. moderately disagree
D. strongly disagree

14. My energy level is higher than that of most people.
A. strongly agree
B. moderately agree
C. moderately disagree
D. strongly disagree

15. I'm able to remain calm and perform well in a crisis.
A. strongly agree
B. moderately agree
C. moderately disagree
D. strongly disagree

16. I can be patient and acknowledge when a situation is be-
yond my control.
A. strongly agree
B. moderately agree
C. moderately disagree
D. strongly disagree

17. I love the challenge of analyzing, attacking, and complet-
ing a complex task.
A. strongly agree
B. moderately agree
C. moderately disagree
D. strongly disagree

18. I've often led and directed projects and groups.
A. strongly agree
B. moderately agree
C. moderately disagree
D. strongly disagree

19. I can easily change course once I've started a project.
A. strongly agree
B. moderately agree
C. moderately disagree
D. strongly disagree

20. I'm capable of firing an unproductive employee, although
I would not be happy at the prospect of doing it.
A. strongly agree
B. moderately agree
C. moderately disagree
D. strongly disagree

21. I like to experiment and try new things—from meeting
new people to trying new activities.
A. strongly agree
B. moderately agree
C. moderately disagree
D. strongly disagree

22. I've had _____ years of experience, either in business or
as a hobby, in the field in which I plan to start a business.
A. more than 3
B. 1 to 3
C. between 6 months and 1
D. 0

23. I've had the following business experience:
A. owned and managed my own business
B. management-level experience (supervised others)
C. employee-level experience (no supervisees)
D. none

24. I've been ill to the extent that it curtailed my activi-
ties _____ days over the past three years.
A. 0 to 5
B. 6 to 10
C. 11 to 15
D. 16 or more

25. I function most effectively if I get at least _____ hours
of sleep a night.
A. 5 or less
B. 6
C. 7
D. 8

INTERPRETING YOUR SCORE

92–100 The Fortune 500 Awaits!

You possess most, if not all, of the key personality and behavioral traits of the successful entrepreneur. Get to work!

84–91 Go For It!

You're no Bill Gates, but you still possess an encouraging
number of entrepreneurial characteristics. If your score on the
last five questions was 23 or above, your behavioral attitudes

could compensate for any personality traits you might be lacking.

75–83 Think Again!

You possess some entrepreneurial traits, but not to the degree needed to buck the odds and be successful. If your score on the last five questions was 22 or below, the risk is even greater. Be honest with yourself. If you feel you can improve in the areas in which you scored poorly, you might be okay. But if you think your weak points are beyond hope, don't take the chance.

Less Than 75 Stay Right Where You Are!

You possess an insufficient number of the personality traits and behavior patterns common to entrepreneurs. But don't feel bad. Harry Truman failed at business, and look what happened to him!

WHAT'S NEXT?

Hopefully, this chapter has helped you get some idea of just how prepared (or unprepared) you are to go into business. If you've come through the chapter's self-analysis with the confidence that you have what it takes, it's time to get down to the nuts and bolts of starting a mail-order business.

The first step is to look at what I call the 12 Rules For Doing It Cheaply. These rules apply to some degree to any mail-order start-up business, but they're absolutely critical to starting one with a minimal investment. We'll take a look at them in chapter 4.

❖**4**❖

THE 12 RULES FOR DOING IT CHEAPLY

One of my goals in this book is to demonstrate how you can start a successful mail-order business for less than $10,000. From this point on, whenever possible, we'll examine the various tasks necessary in starting your business within the context of doing them cheaply. Those sections will be prefaced by a symbol whose message is clear—⑤. Look for them throughout the book. They'll give you a lot more advice on keeping your costs down.

As I pointed out earlier, one of the great things about mail order is that you can make it as cheap and simple or as expensive and complex as you like. Some people start heavily capitalized mail-order businesses with offices, employees, computers, a ton of telecommunications equipment, a warehouse, hefty advertising budgets, and a lot of inventory. They're looking at the big time, and they're making a major investment and putting their futures on the line right from the start.

At the other end of the spectrum are people who start mail-order businesses on a shoestring. They invest anywhere from a few hundred dollars to a few thousand dollars. Some operate part-time, sell just a few items, and are content with whatever business they happen to get. Others operate full-time and work hard to grow their businesses. Sometimes, they achieve unexpected success. Let's look at one mail-order business that started small, is growing quickly, and has followed the 12 rules necessary to keep costs to a minimum.

A MAIL-ORDER STAR IS BORN

I have a friend, Jeannie Johnston, who makes very beautiful and distinctive jewelry. She never tried real hard to market her work, but she always did fairly well selling things at occasional weekend craft fairs and through craft shops in the area. Her earrings, bracelets, and necklaces were reasonably priced between $25 and $75. While she didn't make loads of money, her earnings nicely augmented her husband's salary and gave her the freedom to take care of their two small children.

Then one day a friend suggested to Jeannie that she should try selling her jewelry by mail order.

"Look at the opportunities you're missing," her friend said. "When you go to these craft shows, you're limited to selling your jewelry to the people who visit the shows. But think of all the people who have bought things from you over the years. They like your work and would probably buy more of it. But unless they cross paths with you at one of these shows, they never have the chance. If you send flyers to them, I'll bet they'll buy a few things from you every year."

Jeannie thought about it for a few weeks and finally decided what the heck, it's worth a try. Because she had always kept a guest book at the craft fairs she attended, she already had a mailing list of more than 2,000 names and addresses. She combined her artistic talents with some computer graphics expertise to design a flyer. Since she couldn't afford to have photographs taken of her work, she drew some illustrations. Her husband, a journalist, helped her with some clever advertising copy.

Jeannie knew that if she was going to have any luck at all with her venture, it would come at the holiday season. So on October 19, 1992 (she still remembers the date), she sent out 2,000 flyers. They were nothing fancy, printed on pale yellow 8½-by-11-inch paper and folded to letter size. But the design was attractive, and the illustrations and copy were fairly seductive.

Around two weeks after the mailing, Jeannie got her first response: a bundle of about 100 flyers returned by the post office because of expired forwarding notices and other address problems. She was crushed.

"I thought I had completely wasted my time," she recalls. "After all that effort, all I got was a bunch of returned mail. It was very depressing."

But then, a few days later, she got an order. A pair of earrings and matching necklace. The next day she got three more orders. The day after that, a couple more. By Thanksgiving, she had received more than 30 orders. By the third week of December, the total had reached almost 100, and she'd had two phone calls inquiring about custom-made pieces. She says she worked so hard between Thanksgiving and Christmas, that she barely had time to get her own family's holiday organized.

On New Year's Day, 1993, when things had calmed down, Jeannie sat down to figure out the totals. She'd sold more than 100 pairs of earrings, several dozen necklaces and bracelets, and 20 or so other pieces for a total of nearly $9,000. Plus she was working on the two custom pieces, which would bring in another $500. Since she marks up her jewelry 100 percent from cost, she'd earned almost $4,500, less the cost of the mailing. She was absolutely astonished.

She also discovered she loves making money. In the three years since she sent out her first flyers, she's added nearly 3,000 names to her original mailing list and now sends out three mailings a year. Like Henry Ford, she's discovered the cost-effectiveness of the assembly line, making several dozen of the same item at one time. She has people who help her part-time when business picks up, and she devotes a full forty hours a week to the business. In 1993, she grossed around $22,000. In 1994, she passed $30,000. In 1995, as this book was being written, she expected to reach $45,000.

THE 12 RULES FOR DOING IT CHEAPLY

Jeannie Johnston is like a lot of people who turn hobbies into businesses. She did it on little more than a whim, invested a minimal amount of money, and would have been happy accepting whatever business showed up in the mailbox. In her case, however, unexpected success showed her the potential of mail order. It served as the catalyst for what is now a serious, full-time endeavor.

At the start, like most novices, Jeannie was much better at her hobby than she was at business. She made lots of mistakes, but she learned quickly and has since turned into a savvy businessperson and a firm believer in keeping costs low and sales high. We can use her experience to study the 12 basic rules for starting a mail-order business with minimal investment. She followed some of the rules by accident. She learned the others through experience.

But the bottom line is she started a business that's now approaching $45,000 a year in sales and she's never had more than a few thousand dollars tied up in it at any given time. When we've finished looking at how you can keep your expenses to a minimum, $10,000 will seem like all the money in the world.

⑨ RULE 1—MAKE A BUSINESS PLAN

Every business, no matter its size, needs a business plan. Jeannie didn't have one when she entered the mail-order business with her now infamous holiday mailing, but she does now. And she updates it every fall to prepare for the following year.

A business plan serves as a blueprint for your operation and is critical in controlling costs. A complete business plan will describe the nature of your business, its management, products, production methods, marketing strategies, costs of operation, and projected sales and profits.

If you plan on borrowing money, lenders will insist on examining your business plan. They'll look at your loan application with five things in mind—the nature of the business you're starting; your ability to repay the loan; your financial history; the amount you have to invest; and the value of the collateral you're offering against the loan. The better prepared you are to provide them with this information, the better your chances of getting the money. For this reason, your business plan should be thoroughly thought out, and it should leave no questions unanswered.

Sit down with paper and pencil and plot your strategy for the first year. Where will your business be located? What will you sell? How much will each item cost you? What will you charge for it? How and where will you advertise, and how much will it cost? What will your shipping costs be? What will you need to spend for contracted help? What are your total projected revenues, costs, and profit for the first year?

Obviously, a business plan for a small start-up mail-order business will be a bit less complex than one for, say, the Chrysler Corporation. Still, it's important that it answer all these questions. Your business plan will define your goals, guide you through the year, and serve as a yardstick against which you can measure your progress.

Or lack of progress, as the case may be. Your business plan is also an important tool to help you anticipate failure. You'll know what your monthly costs are going to be and how much business you'll have to do to surpass those costs and be profitable. Sadly, there may come a time when, after too many months of not meeting your expenses, you'll have to admit that things aren't working out and it's time to throw in the towel. (We'll take a more detailed look at business plans in chapter 9.)

⑤ Rule 2—Don't Pay Rent

Jeannie started her business in her home, working in an extra room on the first floor of her house. She plans to stay there as long as possible. Granted, as a jeweler, her space needs are less than someone who makes and sells bean bag chairs. But she's followed the most important rule of starting a mail-order business on the cheap—don't even *think* about leasing an office or other commercial space. Use a spare bedroom, your basement, your attic, your garage, or even a corner of your living room. Right there you've saved thousands of dollars a year.

⑤ Rule 3—Use Your Own Money

You've learned to avoid rent. The next rule is to avoid paying interest. If you can start your business with your savings, by all means do it.

Jeannie did. Her initial investment for her first mailing was less than $700. Of that, $580 was for two thousand 29-cent stamps—an expensive mistake—because she didn't learn about bulk mail permits until it was too late. (We'll look at mailing regulations and costs in chapter 12.) She also figures she had about $600 on hand in inventory and supplies. She has never had to take out a loan.

If you absolutely *have* to borrow money, try to keep it within a range that you're comfortable with and can pay back quickly. One reason for taking out a loan is to purchase inventory. You should obtain a short-term loan that will be paid back as soon as the inventory is sold. The less time you spend in debt, the lower your interest expenses. (We'll look at sources of financing in chapter 5.)

⑨ RULE 4—DON'T HIRE EMPLOYEES

Do as much as you can yourself. If you need to hire help, whether full-time or part-time, treat the people as independent contractors, just as you would an accountant or an attorney. That way, they're responsible for their social security taxes and income taxes, and you avoid a lot of headaches and expense.

For example, let's say you're like Jeannie and need to hire someone during the holiday season. You're paying her seven dollars an hour to process orders and pack boxes. At the end of the week, she has worked twenty-two hours. Because she's an independent contractor, you would simply write her a check for $154. If she was an employee, you'd have to withhold taxes and social security from her check. You'd have to get involved with worker's compensation and unemployment. You'd also have to contribute half of her social security taxes out of *your* pocket.

Given all this, you won't be surprised to learn that the IRS has taken a hard look at the employee versus independent contractor question. Obviously, they prefer people to be employees. Because employees have their taxes withheld by their employers each pay period, the IRS is fairly assured of getting what it's owed. The employers put the withheld taxes aside and then send them in to the IRS each quarter. At least that's what they're *supposed* to do. Those who don't eventually receive a visit from IRS agents and find their businesses padlocked and their assets seized.

Independent contractors, on the other hand, send the IRS a quarterly payment based on what *they* report they earned. And according to the IRS and most economists, there's a huge gap between what's reported and what's really earned. Some estimate this "underground economy" is worth billions of dollars. That's a lot of uncollected taxes.

To keep everyone on their toes, the IRS has established a list of qualifications it uses to distinguish between an employee and an independent contractor. We'll look at them in chapter 13.

⑧ Rule 5—Sell What You Know

This simple rule is why so many people like Jeannie are able to turn their hobbies or interests into successful mail-order businesses. Consider your own interests. What really makes you happy? Are you a golf fanatic? Selling golf accessories would be perfect for you. Or perhaps you love blues music. There are decades' worth of wonderful blues recordings on both LP and compact disc that aren't readily available in most record stores. A mail-order business specializing in hard-to-find blues recordings would let you combine your interests in music and in business.

Sound knowledge of your products is a key to success. You have a responsibility to your customers to provide them with the highest-quality merchandise you can. If you sell them junk, you're not going to be in business very long. Furthermore, if you're buying your merchandise from manufacturers or wholesalers rather than producing it yourself, *you* need to be able to discern quality from junk. If you know what you're looking for, you won't have a problem. But if you're willing to rely on what you're told, I know a guy who has some nice property in Florida you might be interested in.

⑧ RULE 6—MAINTAIN MINIMAL INVENTORY

Maintaining minimal inventory is one of the most important rules in any business, and for one simple reason: *inventory is useless until it's sold.* When inventory is sitting idly on the shelves, it's like having money sitting there. If it's your money, meaning you purchased the inventory with your own capital, it's costing you whatever interest the money could be earning if it were nestled comfortably in an investment account.

If it's someone else's money sitting on the shelves, meaning you *borrowed* the capital to buy the inventory, it's costing you even more. Not only are you losing out on the interest the money could be earning if it were invested but you're also *paying* interest to the lender. It's a double whammy that cuts even further into your profits.

In starting your mail-order business, you need to think of inventory in almost negative terms. Your goal should really be to have *no* inventory on hand. It sounds odd, and I'll admit it's not always possible. But depending on what you sell and where you get your merchandise, you can sometimes manage your inventory in this fashion.

The reason is that, unlike a retail store, you're not dealing face-to-face with your customers. You don't need to have the merchandise sitting on a shelf waiting to be purchased. Your customers are ordering merchandise from you, so there's a built-in time lag between the time you get the order and the time you ship the order. The trick is to not purchase inventory until you have orders for it. Then you're using your customers' money to buy it rather than your own. You're also taking advantage of the fact that many suppliers give you thirty days to pay for your merchandise. When it arrives, move it out as quickly as you can.

It's a delicate process that requires accurate timing and a good relationship with your suppliers. And, again, it's not always possible. But when it is, it's an excellent strategy for minimizing the amount of cash you need to have tied up in the business.

⑧ Rule 7—Cash Only

Maintaining a steady cash flow is critical to any business. When you're trying to operate with a minimum investment of your own, it's even more important. That means accepting only cash, checks, money orders, and credit cards as payment for your merchandise. No credit. No CODs.

⑧ Rule 8—Operate as a Corporation

When you start a business, you can choose to structure it in several ways—a sole proprietorship, a partnership, or a corporation. Each has specific liability and tax ramifications. There are also varying degrees of expense involved.

For a start-up mail-order business—or any business, for that matter—I recommend operating as a corporation. A lot of people might disagree with me, because setting up a corporation is more expensive than establishing a proprietorship or a partnership, running anywhere from $500 to $1,000. You usually have to pay more in taxes as well, and their complexity might cost you a little extra in accountant's fees.

But there's one absolutely critical reason for spending the money—*operating as a corporation protects your personal assets from creditors and legal judgments.* If the business fails or someone successfully sues you, only the assets of the business can be attached. Your personal assets—your house, your car, your bank accounts—will be safe.

A sole proprietorship, on the other hand, leaves you completely vulnerable to financial disaster. Since you are the sole owner of the business, you alone will be responsible for every debt and obligation of the business. If you're sued, your personal assets will be subject to lien to satisfy the claims against you. That means you could lose your savings, your car, and even your house.

What it really comes down to is how much risk you're willing to take and how soundly you want to sleep at night. Granted, if you're operating a small business, carrying little debt, and selling a product that doesn't pose a threat to people's health or safety, your chances of running into trouble are fairly slim. But you never know what lurks around the corner, so sometimes it's better to err on the side of caution.

Jeannie Johnston finally realized this and incorporated her business, even though she has never borrowed money and she never imagined anyone suing her because of a horrible jewelry accident. She had her change of heart when she read an article in the paper about a couple that was suing a toy manufacturer because their toddler son had choked to death on a small toy part.

"That could happen to me if a child choked on a piece of jewelry," she recalls saying to her husband. The next day she called her lawyer.

As you can see, incorporation is important for protection. But the best way to protect yourself is to avoid trouble altogether. This is why the next rule is so important.

$ RULE 9—AVOID LEGAL RISKS

Unfortunately, we live in a very litigious society. Businesses are sued every day for all sorts of things, from making fraudulent claims to selling products that cause personal injury. And people are winning settlements for unbelievable claims. A few years ago, a woman successfully sued McDonald's because she burned herself when she spilled a cup of their coffee on herself *while holding it between her legs in a moving car!* Somehow, a jury decided it was the *restaurant's* fault.

To avoid such hassles, make sure you sell products that don't present a health or safety risk or could otherwise lead to a lawsuit. Also, make sure your advertising is honest and that you don't make any outlandish or unsubstantiated claims.

$ RULE 10—REINVEST IN THE BUSINESS

If you intend to grow your business over time, you're going to need more and more money. The cheapest way to finance your growth is to pour as much of your profits as you can back into the business. Investing your own money will help you avoid having to borrow money.

The best way to accomplish this is to build it into your business plan. Decide ahead of time how much of your earnings you're going to pay yourself in salary. Keep the rest in the business. (Okay, if you have a *really* great year, give yourself a bonus. But don't get carried away.) It may require some sacrifice during the first few years, but that's part of getting a business up and running.

What you *don't* want to do is borrow heavily so you can keep all the profits yourself. If you're more concerned with personal income than the life of your business, you'll put a huge burden on the business that can quickly lead to its failure.

⑧ Rule 11—If You Don't Need It, Don't Buy It

This is a fairly obvious rule for keeping costs down, but it's not always that easy to follow. In the excitement of starting their new entrepreneurial venture, many people get carried away. The next thing you know, they're running around spending money on things they don't really need.

"I need an office!" they'll tell themselves and run out and buy a desk, a chair, filing cabinets, shelves, bulletin boards, a Rolodex, binders, ledgers, spreadsheets, planners, paper clips, staplers, pens, pencils, and all sorts of other junk. They think if they have a well-furnished office, they can't help but be successful.

It's the same mind-set that drives weekend athletes to spend a lot of money on clothing and equipment in an effort to look like the pros. They think it'll make them play better. Believe me, it doesn't work. A friend and I recently played golf with his fifteen-year-old son. The kid was wearing shorts, sneakers, a Hootie and the Blowfish T-shirt, and using a beat-up old set of clubs his grandfather had handed down to him. His father and I were both decked out like Greg Norman and armed with about $1,000 worth of state-of-the-art woods and irons. He kicked our butts.

Just as my fancy equipment didn't help me, all this new office equipment isn't going to help you. You don't need a new chair. You've already got a houseful of chairs. A new desk? Forget it. You must have a desk somewhere in the house. If you don't, use an old table, a card table, or even throw a sheet of plywood over some sawhorses. And as for the filing cabinets, the Rolodex, the ledgers, the spreadsheets, the planner, and the files, you don't need them, either. That's because of rule 12.

⑧ RULE 12—BUY A COMPUTER

After giving you all these rules on how to save money, I'm going to give you one that will require you to spend some. Buy a computer and a printer. They're absolutely essential to running any business.

Once loaded with the appropriate software, your computer will serve as your filing cabinet, storing electronic documents and correspondence. It will be your Rolodex, holding the names and addresses of important business contacts as well as those of the people on your mailing list. It will hold the numbers you'd keep in a ledger. And it will provide you with spreadsheets that will keep track of costs and income and chart your profits.

Your computer will also serve as your daily planner. You'll use it for writing letters and for keeping track of accounts payable and accounts receivable as well your bank accounts. You'll use it to create advertisements with interesting graphics and a variety of typefaces. You'll keep lists of what your customers have purchased over the years. And you'll keep track of inventory, create invoices, and print envelopes, business cards, and mailing labels.

When Jeannie's first holiday mailing proved so successful, she took about $2,500 of the profits and invested in a Macintosh computer and a printer. It's one of the company's cheaper models, but it has plenty of RAM and more than enough hard disk space for her to keep all her business records, including her tax returns, as well as an extensive file of memory-gobbling graphics. She has a spreadsheet package to keep track of income and expenses and a design program she uses to create her flyers. She keeps her mailing list on the computer and uses it to print her mailing labels. She's also loaded a half dozen games on it to keep her kids busy when they're with her in her workroom.

Jeannie's long-range plan is to conduct business electronically as well as through the mail. She's purchased a modem and is learning as much as she can about the Internet, the World Wide Web, HTML (hypertext markup language, the programming language used to compose text on the Web), HTTP (hypertext transfer protocol, the basic tool for formatting text on a Web page), URLs (uniform resource locators, the electronic "addresses" used on the Web), scanning images, and all the other nuances of cyberspace. When she's ready, she plans on designing a home page her customers will see when they visit her electronic address.

WHAT HAPPENS IF YOU GET TOO BIG?

For the owner of a small business, success can be something of a mixed blessing. As your business grows, it can become increasingly harder to adhere to the rules of operating cheaply. It's entirely possible you may eventually need to lease a business space, take out loans, and hire employees. If you haven't already incorporated (and I hope you have), you may find it's time to do so.

But success doesn't mean you have to completely abandon the rules for operating cheaply: you just have to modify them somewhat. If you need to rent space, rent the most inexpensive place you can find that meets your needs. If you need to borrow money, shop around for the best rates you can find, and minimize the length of your loans. The same goes for buying equipment, supplies, and merchandise. Shop around, find the lowest prices, and don't be afraid to haggle a little bit with vendors. It's all part of the game.

You don't have to worry about the problem of success yet. You haven't even started your business. Just realize that the bottom line in all this is the health of *your* bottom line. Minimizing expenses is a critical aspect of operating your business. The other is maximizing income. By carefully planning for both, you can enjoy growth and profits.

WHAT'S NEXT?

Now that we've looked at the 12 Rules For Doing It Cheaply, we'll take a more detailed look at getting a mail-order business off the ground. You'll need to decide what you're going to sell, where to get your merchandise, and whether or not you'll need financing. You'll need to determine who and where your customers are, learn how to test the market to see if your choices are viable, find out all about postal regulations, and plan your marketing strategies. You'll also need to figure out what kind of equipment you're going to need and set up a system for processing and mailing out your orders.

❧5❧

FINANCING YOUR BUSINESS

Deciding to make the commitment is always the first big hurdle in starting a business. The second is finding the money to pay for it.

Obtaining financing is typically *the* biggest challenge facing any new business, and mail order is no exception. If you're lucky, you may not need much money. If you're starting small, your needs may be fairly minimal. And if you've managed to put together a nice chunk of cash, you can use that to start your business. But if you're like most of us, you're going to be going hat in hand to lenders and asking for a loan.

This may not be something you're looking forward to. As we learned in chapter 3, running a business will require you to perform many tasks, and few people are comfortable with all of them. If dealing with money is something you're not particularly fond of, you're going to have to learn to persevere and get it done. This is a perfect place to start.

TIME FOR A REALITY CHECK

Before we discuss some of the sources you might tap to finance your business, you might as well hear the bad news. *You're not going to get any money from institutional lenders*. No way. No how. End of discussion. Don't even think about it.

Why? Because entrepreneurs are rarely able to get start-up funds from banks. These are very conservative institutions that don't like to take risks. And there's nothing more risky to a banker than a bright-eyed entrepreneur with a lot of ideas and an empty wallet.

But don't dismay. This simply means you're going to have to be creative if you want to come up with the money. It's not a problem. There are many sources other than banks out there. We'll take a look at them in a minute. But before we do, let's figure out exactly how much money you're going to need.

DETERMINE HOW MUCH YOU'LL NEED

Before you start looking for money, you'll need to know what your total costs are going to be. Let's say you're starting a mail-order business selling golf balls personalized with people's initials, business logo, or other identifiers. We'll assume you're following the 12 Rules For Doing It Cheaply and operating your business at home. We'll also assume you're going the bare-bones route with furnishings and using stuff you have around the house. Right off the bat, you've saved a lot of money by not paying rent and not spending money on office furnishings. Allow a few bucks for a calculator, some pens and paper, and other miscellaneous office supplies. You'll also have some fees for professional services and incorporating the business.

Next, we'll spend some money where it's needed, on equipment (start-up equipment needs are discussed in chapter 8). You'll need a computer and a printer, some software, and a combination telephone and answering machine. We'll forget about a fax machine for the moment. You can get one down the road if you feel it's really necessary. You'll also need the proper equipment to stamp the golf balls, and a variety of paints.

The next consideration is inventory. Golfers are very particular about the type of ball they play, so you'll need to carry the most popular half dozen brands. And to get the best price from manufacturers, you'll need to buy quite a few at a time. This means your initial outlay for inventory will be pretty high. Then you'll need a few hundred dollars for shipping materials, stationery, and business cards. You'll also spend a few bucks to have a logo designed.

That leaves just advertising costs. Your market research (we'll discuss this in detail in chapter 7) has shown that the best way to advertise your product is with a small ad in the back of the golf magazines. It's a lot more expensive than the newspaper classifieds, but it's clearly the best way to reach your customers (we'll look at advertising options in chapter 10).

We'll add everything up to see how much you're going to need.

EXPENSE	COST
Business license	50.00
Other fees	50.00
Insurance	
Home	300.00
Equipment	Covered by homeowner's policy
Professional consultation	
Attorney fees, including incorporation	750.00
Accountant fees	200.00
Office expenses	
Calculator	15.00
Miscellaneous (pens, paper, etc.)	50.00
Equipment	
Telephone	75.00
Answering machine	75.00
Computer	1,900.00
Software	100.00
Printer	275.00
Ball stamper, paint, etc.	225.00
Inventory	3,000.00
Shipping materials	
Boxes	200.00
Tape	50.00
Miscellaneous	50.00

Advertising/Promotion
   Letterhead 100.00
   Business cards 25.00
   Logo design 50.00
   Advertising (2 months)..1,800.00

TOTAL COSTS $9,340.00

We've managed to keep your costs just under $10,000. As you can see, aside from your computer, which is really a fixed cost, your two biggest expenses are inventory and advertising. This is why minimizing inventory and selecting the proper advertising venue are so important.

COVER YOUR LIVING EXPENSES

Don't forget, you'll still have a family to support while you're building your business, so you need to have enough cash left over to meet expenses. Many business experts recommend that you have from six months' to a year's worth of income set aside to tide you over until the business begins to run smoothly. One seasoned business adviser I know tells his clients, "Assume you're not going to make a penny the first year and plan accordingly."

   How much will you need? Obviously, it depends on your monthly living costs, the number of children you have, and many other factors. To get a ballpark figure of how much you'll need to get by for a year, fill in your monthly costs in this chart and then figure your annual total.

Rent/mortgage payment	_____ × 12 =	_____
Gas & electric	_____ × 12 =	_____
Telephone	_____ × 12 =	_____
Food	_____ × 12 =	_____
Clothing	_____ × 12 =	_____
Car payment(s)	_____ × 12 =	_____

Insurance	_____	× 12 =	_____
Gasoline	_____	× 12 =	_____
Entertainment	_____	× 12 =	_____
Taxes	_____	× 12 =	_____
Debt payment	_____	× 12 =	_____
Tuition	_____	× 12 =	_____
Medical	_____	× 12 =	_____
Other	_____	× 12 =	_____

TOTAL   _____

This will give you a rough idea of what you and your family will need to survive for the first year you're in business. Just to be on the safe side, it might not be a bad idea to throw in another couple of thousand dollars for unexpected emergencies.

WHERE TO LOOK

Now that you know how much you'll need to get started, you can begin to consider different sources of financing. You'll be surprised at how many resources are out there.

⑤ YOUR SAVINGS

We might as well start with the obvious. If you've managed to put aside a little nest egg, it's time to put it to work. Whatever cash you have on hand, any securities you may own, even IRAs and other savings plans—these can all be tapped to raise cash. Granted, in the case of retirement savings plans, you'll pay a penalty for early withdrawal of funds. But the important thing is the money's there if you decide you need it.

HOME EQUITY LOANS

Home equity loans, which are really just second mortgages cloaked in a less threatening name, are becoming one of the most popular forms of financing for all sorts of things—cars, home renovations, college tuition. They're also excellent sources of financing for small business start-ups.

This is one situation where a bank will be happy to see you come through the door. They like home equity loans because there's virtually no risk involved. If the borrower defaults on the loan, the bank has a very tangible asset—the borrower's home—to back up the loan. Let's say your home is worth $150,000 and your mortgage balance is $50,000. That means you have $100,000 worth of equity in your home. You can borrow against that equity—usually up to 70 percent of its value—to finance your business. As we learned earlier, however, the downside is serious. You're literally betting your house on your success. If the business fails, you may suddenly find yourself without a roof over your head.

Approach your search for a home equity loan just the way you did for your first mortgage. Call the commercial banks, credit unions, and savings and loans in your area to shop around for interest rates. Are they offering fixed-rate or variable-rate loans? If they're variable-rate, how is the rate adjusted and what is the cap? Are there additional up-front fees you'll have to pay? Will you have to pay "points," a percentage of the principal (usually one to three percent), at the beginning of the loan? Remember to add any fees paid at the beginning of the loan to your total start-up costs.

Check with your accountant to see if you should get the kind of loan where you pay off some of the principal each month or the kind where you just pay off the interest each month and then pay back the principal in a giant "balloon" payment at the end of the loan. But remember, if you don't have the cash to make that last payment, you'll have to refinance.

Approach home equity loans with extreme caution. They can be a great resource. They can also drag you into financial ruin. If you're like most people, your home is your most precious asset. If you're going to risk it to finance your business, do your homework very, very carefully to make sure your business will earn enough to cover the monthly payments.

⑤ Find a Partner

You may have a friend or relative who's interested in becoming a partner in the business. He'll put up a percentage of the money in return for part ownership of the business and a percentage of the annual profits. It can be a very lucrative investment.

The way the two of you decide to operate the business will determine how the profits are shared. If he's involved in another business, he may wish to be a silent partner and let you be responsible for running the show.

Let's use my friend Steve as an example. Steve is a college professor who for years has invested in all sorts of things, including a few small businesses. He's been quite successful and has made impressive amounts of money. In fact, his earnings from his business interests long ago surpassed those from his teaching.

Over the years, he and I have talked about starting a business that I would run. Let's say we both put up half the money, $5,000 each, so we each own half the business. But since I'm the one running the business day to day, we agree I'll get 90 percent of the operating profits.

The first year, the business nets $20,000. My portion would be $18,000, and his would be $2,000. That's a 40 percent return on his investment, a great deal in anyone's book. And over the long term, he can really make some money. If the business performs well and grows steadily, we might be able to sell it down the road for many times our initial investment. Since he owns half the business, half the profit would be his.

There are many other ways partnerships can be set up. Each has different legal considerations and requires the expertise of an attorney experienced in business partnerships.

There are also downsides to partnerships. The biggest problem comes from the fact that there are always two or more people involved in making decisions. If everyone has a different idea about how things should be handled, the business can go down the tubes while everyone's trying to get their own way. For this reason, it's critical that the responsibilities and authority of all the partners be defined in the partnership agreement before the business is started.

⑧ YOUR PERSONAL ASSETS

Take a look around you. If you're over thirty, you've probably begun to amass a fair amount of stuff. If you're over forty, your house might look like a garage sale waiting to happen. If you're like me, you have an amazing amount of junk that's sitting around unused. It's all worth something to somebody.

Unloading unused personal items is an excellent way to raise cash. People do it all the time, in the classifieds, by having garage sales, in the newsletter at work. And it's amazing how much it can be worth. Last summer, my neighbors across the street had a garage sale after their last child moved out of the house. They raised almost $3,000 in two days. There's your inventory money!

⑧ SEVERANCE PACKAGES

If you've fallen victim to the rash of corporate "restructurings" that have become so common in American industry, you may have received a handsome chunk of cash as part of your severance package. Many companies give their employees up to a year's pay plus unused vacation and sick time. That money can be an excellent source of financing for your business.

⑧ FRIENDS AND RELATIVES

Friends and relatives are frequently an excellent source of financing, not just for businesses but also for homes, automobiles, and other big-ticket items. It can be an excellent deal for you both, because of the gap that exists between current lending rates and the interest rates that institutions are offering on savings accounts, certificates of deposit, and other savings products.

Let's say your mother has $10,000 to invest. She's ultra-conservative, so she doesn't want to fool around with mutual funds or other more risky forms of investment. She looks at various fixed-rate investments and discovers she can earn around 4.5 percent with a conventional savings account and in the neighborhood of 6 percent with most CDs.

In the meantime, you just happen to be looking for $10,000

to finance your business. She has confidence in your talents (she is your mom, after all) and agrees to loan you the $10,000 at 8 percent. You're both quite happy. She's getting a better return on her money, and you're getting the money you need to start your business. It works out great for you both.

There are some drawbacks to borrowing money from friends and relatives. First, if the business fails, you're going to have a pretty hard time telling your mother you lost her money. You might find that your friend or relative might at some point decide they have the right to tell you how to run the business. Also, money has a way of destroying relationships. Making sure all the contingencies are thought out, agreed upon beforehand, and put in writing can save a lot of agony later on.

Credit Cards

Have you checked your mail lately? If you're like me, you're constantly getting offers for VISA cards, MasterCards, and other credit cards at special introductory rates. The banks sponsoring the cards offer low interest rates, say 5 to 7 percent, on purchases and cash advances for the first six months you have the card. After six months, the interest rate on the balance and subsequent purchases and cash advances jumps up to the more standard 16 to 19 percent.

If you're getting these offers, you're being provided a whole bunch of opportunities for short-term financing at very attractive interest rates. Let's say you need to raise $10,000 to finance your business, and you have all these offers of pre-approved credit lines of $5,000. You find a couple of banks that will give you a 5.9 percent interest rate for six months, take them up on their offers of credit cards, and take out the entire amount in cash advances. Suddenly you have your $10,000. At the end of the six-month introductory period, if you still have outstanding debt on the cards, you can take two new banks up on their credit card offers, pay off your balances with the first two banks, and maintain your low interest rate. If the number of solicitations I receive is any indication of what most people are receiving, you could operate this way for years.

⑤ LIFE INSURANCE POLICIES

If you have a whole life insurance policy or some other policy that builds equity, you're sitting on an excellent source of financing. These policies usually allow you to take out loans against the cash value they've accrued over the years. And in many cases, you only have to pay quarterly or semiannual interest payments on the loan. You also might be able to get the insurance company itself to provide you with financing, using your life insurance policy as collateral.

BE PREPARED

I have a friend who's a commercial loan officer for a bank. I once asked him where people applying for business loans go wrong when they come in to see him. His answer?

They're unprepared.

"I can't tell you how many times someone has come into my office, told me a little bit about the business they want to buy, and then dumped a whole pile of paper on my desk and said, 'Well, whaddaya think?' " he said. "It's amazing. They expect me to do their homework for them."

When you approach someone for a loan—whether it's a banker or a friend or relative—you must be prepared to present him a well thought out analysis of the business. You'll need to tell him how you intend to use the money you'll be borrowing and show him that the business will perform well enough to pay him back. Throwing a pile of paper at him and suggesting that maybe *he* figure it all out is not going to get you your loan.

Remember, you're asking him for his hard-earned cash. He's going to want to know the exact nature of the business, how much money it will generate, and how you plan to generate it. Most importantly, he's going to want you to prove to him how it will make enough money to pay off the loan.

This is where your business plan comes in. It will give the lender this information and give him a complete overview of your business. Your plan should include the following items:

- Overview of the business
- Description of the product or service
- Development plans
- Description of the target market
- Marketing strategy
- Management structure
- Financial information
- Legal information
- Supporting information

When you visit the lender, present him with your business plan. If he allows you the time, go through it item by item. He'll grill you about everything he can think of, so be prepared to answer a lot of questions. Don't try to bluff him if you don't know the answers. Tell him you don't know but you'll get him the information as soon as possible. (We'll look at business plans in more detail in chapter 9.)

WHAT'S NEXT?

Obtaining financing is one big step in getting your mail-order business up and running. Equally important is deciding what to sell. And as we learned in chapter 2, almost anything is viable, as long as you can get it to your customers.

In chapter 6, we'll look at how to evaluate different candidate products for their market potential, how to determine costs, how to calculate earnings potential, and what the other important factors are that you'll need to consider in deciding what products or services you're going to sell.

FOR MORE INFORMATION

There are many books and other sources of information on financing a business. Here are a few good ones:

- *How to Negotiate a Business Loan* by Richard C. Belew (Van Nostrand Reinhold, New York, 1979).

- *Steps to Small Business Financing,* published by the American Bankers Association. Call 202-663-5111.

- *Start-up Money: Raise What You Need for Your Small Business* by Jennifer Lindsey (John Wiley & Sons, 1989).

- *Raising Seed Money for Your Own Business* by Brian Smith (Viking, 1984).

- *Free Money: For Small Businesses & Entrepreneurs* by Laurie Blum (John Wiley & Sons, 1989).

- *Start Your Own Business for $1,000 or Less* by Will Davis (Upstart, 1995).

WHAT WILL YOU SELL?

T here are literally thousands of different products and services being sold in the mail-order industry. While some are extensions of people's hobbies, like Jeannie Johnston's jewelry business, others have been selected simply because a savvy businessperson recognized a good business opportunity.

Some mail-order businesses serve large markets that include broad segments of the population. Others are targeted to very small, carefully defined niche markets. What they all have in common is the fact that they fill customers' needs or satisfy their desires. And as we'll see, that's the key to the marketability of any product or service.

UNDERSTANDING CONSUMER BEHAVIOR

Before you begin to evaluate different products, you need to spend a bit of time studying consumer behavior. Why do people buy the things they do? What factors contribute to their willingness to part with their hard-earned money, particularly for items that are basically useless?

Consider something like the Pet Rock, for example, which had its fifteen minutes of fame back in the late seventies. Dreamed up by an advertising copywriter who was sitting around having a beer after work one day, the Pet Rock was nothing more than an egg-sized rock that was sold in its own little cardboard "rock house" and accompanied by a pamphlet describing its care and feeding.

Dumb idea, right? Well, something about that dumb idea sparked the public's imagination and caused an unbelievable buying frenzy in the United States. People got Pet Rocks for Christmas, for their birthdays, for wedding anniversaries, and for just about every other occasion imaginable. They had Pet Rocks sitting on their desks at work and on their bookshelves at home. They carried them around in their purses and brief-cases. Major news magazines and television shows did stories on the Pet Rock. Like most fads, it didn't last long, maybe five or six months, but that was long enough to make the adman who dreamed it up a very wealthy fellow.

The Pet Rock fell into that broad category of products known as "novelty" items. You know the kind of stuff I'm talking about—the rubber vomit, the whoopee cushion, the dribble glass, the arrow-through-the-head. They're things that make us laugh (well, some of us, anyway) and provide a bit of diversion from the day-to-day routine of our lives. They also fulfill one of our basic desires—*to be entertained*—and that's why they're successful. Here are some other reasons why people buy certain products or services.

PEOPLE WANT TO BE ATTRACTIVE

Like it or not, we live in a culture that rewards beauty and frowns upon ugliness. So you'll never go broke servicing the human ego.

People want to look their best for a variety of reasons—to attract a mate, to get a better job, to be in style, to boost their self-confidence, to be popular with their friends and coworkers, and just to feel better about themselves. It's a universal human need, and it opens the door to all sorts of products, from cos-metics and clothing to vitamins and weight-loss programs.

PEOPLE WANT TO BE HEALTHY

The United States is in the midst of a health and fitness boom. As people have come to realize the benefits of exercise and proper nutrition, the market for products and services that pro-vide them has also grown.

The last fifteen years have seen an explosion in health clubs, health food stores, and home exercise equipment. More and more people have taken up running, biking, swimming, skiing, martial arts, and other sports. They've altered their eating habits, avoiding fat and eating less meat and more fruits and vegetables. In fact, vegetarianism is at an all-time high. This is a trend that shows no sign of slowing down, particularly as baby boomers continue to age. Products and services that keep them physically fit are excellent choices for both retailers and mail-order firms.

People Want to Have More Leisure Time

Americans are busier than ever, and they're more than willing to spend money on goods and services that help them enjoy their leisure time. They'll hire people to clean their homes, take care of their lawns, repair their houses and cars, walk their dogs, and do many other chores. Any product that can save a step around the house can't help but be successful.

People Want to Relive Their Youth

Most of us are incredibly nostalgic, particularly for the years that took us from puberty through young adulthood. The emotions we experienced and the fun we had make those times very special. As a result, everything from those years—the music we listened to, the clothes we wore, the cars we drove—evokes intense emotion.

A perfect example of this occurred as this book was being written. On Sunday, November 19, 1995, twenty-five years after the band broke up, Beatlemania struck the United States all over again. ABC began a three-night, six-hour television special. A new anthology of previously unreleased Beatles music, including two new songs recorded by the surviving Beatles, hit the market the following day. The Sunday *New York Times Magazine* had a full-page ad offering plate-signed, limited edition lithographs of all the Beatles' album covers, for $49.95 each. Beatles memorabilia became hotter than ever. The money was flying!

This wonderful human trait extends far beyond music. Almost anything that reminds people of a treasured time in their lives can be a viable product, and this fact opens the doors to all sorts of niche markets, including even bowling shirts, as we learned in chapter 2.

PEOPLE WANT TO LEARN

Curiosity is another human trait that won't go away. People like learning new things, so the market for new information will always be there. And the market isn't limited to certain age groups or socioeconomic groups. Almost anyone is a potential customer.

There will certainly be no shortage of things for them to learn. We live in a time when the volume of human knowledge is doubling every ten years. The pace of technological development alone is breathtaking. This opens the market for all sorts of books, mail-order educational courses, software programs, compact discs, and other educational products. As baby boomers age, this will be a particularly attractive market.

PEOPLE WANT TO BE SUCCESSFUL

Success is part of the American dream, and most of us are always looking for an edge that will help us get ahead. As a result, products and services aimed at helping people become more successful are a multimillion dollar industry in the United States.

For many people, self-improvement is the goal. They want to shore up some part of their personality they perceive as being inadequate. For example, some people, particularly those in business, want to become more assertive and outgoing. For years, the Dale Carnegie Institute has been taking advantage of this by teaching people how to comfortably meet new acquaintances, work the crowd at social gatherings, speak before groups of people, and develop other social skills they need in their personal and professional lives. The company's success has spawned an entire industry based on teaching people to be more self-confident.

Other products and services are aimed at improving people's professional skills. I work in an office that includes other writers, editors, graphic designers, and marketing people. Every day, our mail includes advertising for publications, seminars, home study courses, video- and audiocassettes, and many other products designed to help us become better at what we do.

People Want to Make Money

This desire isn't too far removed from the desire to be successful. For many people, success and wealth go hand-in-hand, so products and services that help them earn more money are always surefire winners. In fact, if you stop and think about it, you bought this book to learn how to make money.

SELECTING A PRODUCT

Finding a product for your mail-order business is not something that should be taken lightly or rushed into. Your success hinges on what you decide to sell, so you need to take the time to do it right. Here are some of the best ways to find good ideas. We'll begin with some of the best ways of finding *cheap* ideas.

⑤ Start with a Single Product

This is a key to getting started cheaply. Find one product and devote all your energy to building the business around it. Offering a single product is also the safest way to operate when you're just getting your feet wet in the business. As you learn more and the business begins to grow, you can begin to consider additional products.

⑤ Produce the Product Yourself

There are several advantages to this approach. First of all, since you're producing the product, you can control costs by tailoring production to demand. Second, it gives you maximum control over your product. If you find you need to make some adjustments to meet the desires of your customers, you can do so without any problem. This would not be the case if you were selling a product produced by a manufacturer.

Some of the most popular products for the mail-order novice are informational or how-to publications. People are always looking for advice on how to do things like buy or sell a house or a car, repair their credit, find the cheapest air fares, take care of their pets, or earn money from their hobby.

These don't have to be book-length works. Many mail-order entrepreneurs have found amazing success with small, inexpensive pamphlet-sized publications that provide information on all sorts of things. You can write it yourself, and with a little practice with a design program, even design it yourself on your computer.

Because producing your own product is such a good way to get started in the mail-order business, my next suggestion is an obvious strategy.

$ MAKE YOUR HOBBY YOUR BUSINESS

Jeannie Johnston was lucky. In starting her mail-order jewelry business, she turned what was little more than a hobby into a thriving business venture. She's not alone. Many, many people have converted their hobbies and interests into moneymaking mail-order ventures. They're happy because they're dealing in something they know and love and are able to share their interest with other people.

Most business experts, and I'm one of them, highly recommend this approach for people who are entering the mail-order business. It's inexpensive, enables you to exert maximum control over your product or products, and most importantly, allows you to spend your time working in a field you love.

$ FIND A PRODUCT THAT CAN BE DROP-SHIPPED

We learned in chapter 4 that one of the keys to starting a mail-order business cheaply is to keep your inventory levels as low as possible. A drop-ship arrangement is the perfect way to do just that.

What is a drop-ship arrangement? It's one in which a manu-facturer sells you a product, but rather than shipping you the product, he agrees to ship your orders for you himself. Usually, all you need to do is provide him with a shipping label and payment for the order. Since you're receiving payment with the order from your customer, you can immediately pay the manufacturer. That virtually eliminates the need for capital for inventory.

The one downside to the drop-shipment arrangement is you're limited to selling the products of manufacturers who will agree to join you in such an arrangement, so you might not be able to sell exactly what you want. Still, there are quite a few such manufacturers out there, so you will have some choices. We'll discuss the drop-ship arrangement again later in the book.

⑤ Sell Products on Consignment

Selling on consignment is a wonderful way to keep your costs down. When you sell by consignment, you don't have to pay the supplier for merchandise until you sell it. And anything you don't sell can be returned.

Depending on what you're interested in selling, finding con-ventional distributors that will work with you in this manner may be difficult. You'll have better luck selling the work of independent craftspeople—potters, jewelers, fabric artists—and other people who manufacture and market their own products.

Go With What's Already Proven Successful

Have you ever heard the old saying Imitation is the sincerest form of flattery? Well, in mail order, it's a fact of life.

One of the odd truths of the industry is that quite often the best way to be successful is to sell the same products and services that other mail-order businesses are selling. When there are a lot of businesses selling the same product, it means the product has a proven track record of marketability.

This approach may fly in the face of your gut instincts. Many entrepreneurs, both in and out of mail order, get excited by innovation. They think if they come up with a novel product, the world will beat a path to their doorstep. Although there's certainly some truth to this "build a better mousetrap" concept, bringing a new product to market is usually expensive and always risky.

For this reason, as a newcomer to the mail-order business, you're much better off selling a product or service that's already been proven successful. It's easier to let someone else go through the trial and error, the expense, and, frequently, the failure of marketing something new. If it's not going to work, let them spend the time and the money to find out. But once a product has proven successful, it's easy for you to jump on the bandwagon with your own version.

Now, I'm not saying this is a foolproof method of making money in mail order. It still requires that you carefully test-market the product; moreover, the competition will keep you on your toes with your advertising. But if you do your research thoroughly (which we'll discuss in the next chapter), going with a popular product is one of the best strategies you can take.

CHECK MAGAZINES AND NEWSPAPERS

The backs of magazines and newspapers are chock-full of mail-order advertisements for all sorts of products. They run the gamut from the more highbrow publications such as *The New Yorker,* which has ads for fine jewelry, clothing, and furniture, to tabloid sheets like the *Star* and its ads for the services of psychics and astrologers.

Take the time to go through as many magazines and newspapers as you can. And don't just look at the ads—check out the classifieds as well. You'll be amazed at the things people buy. You'll also begin to see patterns in the ads. There *are* certain products that crop up time and time again. You'll also begin to recognize the names and ads of some of the biggest companies in the industry. These may give you some ideas for products or services you'd be interested in selling.

If there are products that interest you, send away for any free information or sample products that their companies may offer. You might even want to purchase a few items to see what the merchandise is really like. If you're worried about spending the money, just make sure you select companies with money-back guarantees. After you've examined the products, all you have to do is return the items. You're only out the money it costs you to send them back. If you really want to keep your costs down, return the items COD. Many companies will accept them.

Study Your Own Mail

If you're like me, you get lots of catalogs and other direct mail solicitations in the mail each week. Save them and study them. Start files and group them according to product. After a while you'll start to see that some files are larger than others. As with perusing the backs of magazines and newspapers, this will give you some idea of what products have the strongest markets.

Within each product file, create smaller groupings organized by price. This will give you some ideas of the price range that exists for a given product or products. As the files grow, you'll even be able to see what price levels are most popular.

For example, suppose you've created a file of ads for men's golf sweaters. Within that file, you've grouped the ads by price, using $10 increments. After a while, you see that sweaters in the $60 to $70 range are the most frequently advertised. This is not an accident. It means that through their own trial and error, the companies selling golf sweaters have found that this is the most popular price range. It offers the best combination of consumer appeal and profitability.

From Storefront to Mail Order

Perhaps you're already running a retail store and would like to expand into mail order. You might even want to convert the business completely to mail order. You wouldn't be the first person to follow this path. Many mail-order businesses—including one of the nation's biggest, Eddie Bauer—began as storefront operations.

From a cost standpoint, expanding into mail order is easily done. You already have a place to do business and the inventory to back you up, so the two biggest costs are covered. Beyond that, you need to acquire a mailing list that would allow you to expand your customer base beyond those who already come to your business; put together a catalog or brochure; and make sure you're prepared to deal with the logistics of mailing out your merchandise. If business warrants, you may even have to hire an extra person or two just to deal with the mail-order side of your business.

Many retailers who have expanded into mail order report that the move helped increase their in-store sales. This is usually due to the higher visibility the store enjoys because of the printed material it's now distributing. The material allows people outside a store's normal market area to learn about the business. Then when they find themselves in the vicinity, they're likely to stop by. A good example of this is the huge number of people who, when visiting New England, make the pilgrimage to L. L. Bean's retail store in Freeport, Maine.

The boost to in-store sales can also help cover the costs of starting up a mail-order operation. If the mail-order business is slow to get out of the gate, the fact that in-store sales have increased can allow the mail-order portion of the business to operate at a loss for a time without hurting the overall profitability of the business.

Most retailers who completely convert to mail order do so only after first adding mail order to their retail operation and building that portion of the business to the point where it's viable on its own. To do otherwise is very risky because it's really like starting an entirely new business from scratch.

⑤ FROM STOREFRONT TO THE INTERNET

Jim Spitznagel of Ithaca, New York, followed his hobby into mail order by way of retailing. The Pittsburgh native had always loved music and began amassing a huge record collection while still in junior high school. He also played in bands. But like a lot of would-be rock stars, "I realized I could play the record player a lot better than I could play the guitar," he jokes.

In 1977, he turned his passion for music into Jim's Records, a successful record store on Liberty Avenue near Carnegie-

Mellon University in Pittsburgh. His broad selection and ency-
clopedic knowledge of music made his shop popular with a
wide range of music lovers, and it was voted the best record
store in Pittsburgh five times during the eighteen years he
owned it.

In 1995, Jim moved to Ithaca, a bustling college town at the
foot of Cayuga Lake in New York's Finger Lakes region. He
wanted to get back in the record business, but the day-to-day
hassles of running a retail shop no longer interested him. What
did catch his fancy was mail order. But it wasn't the kind of
mail order that's been practiced since the earliest days of Sears.
It was mail order with a new twist.

Rather than printing catalogs and buying mailing lists, Jim
opened his business, Jim's Ithaca Music Shop, on the Internet,
the global web of computer networks that links millions of
personal computers. His customers visit his business by using
one of the popular software programs such as Netscape that
allow people to navigate cyberspace. By keyboarding Jim's
electronic address into their computers—or following a link
from another site on the Internet—they're connected to his
home page. Once there, they can flip through additional pages
to peruse his electronic catalog and then place an order using
a credit card. If they have questions, his phone number, his E-
mail address, and his "snail mail" address (his street address
in Ithaca for anyone who wants to communicate with him via
the U.S. mail) are included on his home page.

Jim's business is just one of thousands that have sprung up
on the Internet in just the last couple of years. There will soon
be thousands more, and for very good reason. Starting an electronic business is relatively inexpensive (it's cheaper to create
and update a home page than to print a catalog, and there are
no postal charges), it provides access to literally millions of
customers, and it can be open twenty-four hours a day, seven
days a week.

The technology is about to revolutionize the way we buy and
sell goods and services. Will it replace traditional mail order?
No, at least not anytime soon. But as more and more people
come on-line and become accustomed to buying merchandise

from electronic storefronts, it will certainly become a viable part of the industry and one you should seriously investigate. In chapter 11, we'll take a more detailed look at Jim's business and operating an electronic mail-order business.

TAKE A LOOK AT THE PAST

Sometimes you can find a good product for the future by looking to the past. People's tastes are cyclical, and something that was popular years ago may well pop up again.

Some of the best examples are clothing styles. Look at how the width of men's jacket lapels and ties have widened and narrowed over the years. I noticed just the other day that pleated pants are suddenly out, and plain front pants are coming back. Designers have recently been resurrecting the hip-hugging bell-bottoms that were so popular in the hippie heydays of the late sixties and early seventies. And much to the delight of orthopedic surgeons everywhere, the platform shoe (all you cultural anthropologists may want to see John Travolta in 1974's *Saturday Night Fever* as a reference) has been making a comeback. In fashion, there are only so many ways you can tweak a garment. That's why what goes around always comes around.

One of the best ways to get ideas for old products is to look at back issues of magazines. Go the library and find magazines from the forties, fifties, and sixties, and look at the ads for different products. You never know what might inspire you.

BUY AN EXISTING BUSINESS

Buying an existing business has always been a viable option for people wanting to go into all sorts of businesses. Obviously, if you're looking to start a mail-order business on a shoestring, it's not the way to go. But if you have some money to invest and a good source of financing lined up, it might be worth looking around to see what's out there.

There are some advantages. First of all, your product has already been selected and has established a track record of successful marketability. Second, all the organizational work has already been done. You have mailing lists, equipment, inventory, and the system in place to process orders. And third, you have a long list of (hopefully) repeat customers. All you have to do is write a check and take over.

But writing that check is also the downside to buying an existing business. If you find a good one that shows a history of profitability and lots of promise for the future, it's going to cost you a fair amount of money. The seller, by virtue of his own hard work, has created a thriving enterprise, and he's going to be looking to cash in on it. It's called goodwill—the fact that the business has a track record of profitability. And the more successful it's been, the more he's going to want for it.

Buy a Franchise

This is another popular strategy for many people entering business today. Franchising offers a proven product, a sound marketing system, and the ongoing support of the franchisor who sells you the franchise. This is why franchising is one of the premier growth industries in the United States at the moment. If you do your homework when looking at franchise opportunities, you can find very good companies that will provide you with a solid future.

Once again, though, the downside is money. Buying a franchise is kind of like buying a prefabricated house. Everything's already been cut to fit. All you need to do is put the pieces together. But since other people have already done the work, you're going to have to pay them for their efforts. And the cost goes beyond what you'd pay to buy an established business. Franchising is an ongoing relationship between franchisor and franchisee. After you buy the franchise, you're going to be paying the franchisor a percentage of your sales each month in royalty fees for as long as you own the franchise.

EVALUATING PRODUCTS

Just because a mail-order business already exists doesn't mean that it has a foolproof product or products. The same thing goes for a franchise. What's been successful for the last ten years isn't necessarily going to be successful for the next ten. People's tastes change, markets come and go, and products fall in and out of popularity.

You can't always rely on your hobbies, either. The fact that you're interested in something doesn't mean enough other people share your interest to make it a viable mail-order offering.

This means that when you're looking at potential products or services—whether you're starting your own mail-order business or buying an existing business—you'll need to carefully evaluate them. Here are the critical questions you'll need to ask.

HOW MUCH OF AN INVESTMENT WILL THE PRODUCT REQUIRE?

This is the biggest question of all, so you might as well answer it right off the bat. Is this a product you can afford to sell? Remember, you need inventory, no matter how minimal, and that's going to require a certain amount of cash. Obviously, the higher the unit price of the product, the more money you're going to need. You might as well figure out now if you can afford the product, rather than waste your time analyzing it from all these other angles.

IS THE MARKET FOR THE PRODUCT IN GROWTH OR DECLINE?

Let's consider golf once again, and look at me as a fairly typical golf consumer. (I'll probably bore you with this topic throughout the book, but bear with me. I love the sport, and it's a good example of a thriving mail-order market.)

I'm a certified golf fanatic. I try to play three or four times a week during the season, which, because I live in upstate New York, is only from mid-April through October. During the winter, when I can't play on a course, I play electronic golf on my computer and practice putting in my family room. I read about golf, think about golf, and talk about golf with my buddies. And most importantly, I spend a lot of money on golf.

For the golf industry, this is great news, because I'm just the tip of the iceberg. There are millions of other golf fanatics out there, and our numbers are growing. Golf is a boom market. And because it's a sport all of us aging baby boomers can play until the moment we go to that big clubhouse in the sky, it will continue to be a boom market for the foreseeable future. New courses are being opened at a record pace, new equipment companies enter the market every year, and the market is ripe for novel golf-related products.

Does it Fit a Niche Market Within a Larger Market?

Many times, a hot market can be divided into smaller markets. For example, I currently receive three or four golf equipment catalogs in the mail. I also recently started hearing from several companies that specialize in golf-related gifts and accessories— clothing, monogrammed golf balls, highball glasses, framed prints of famous golf courses, that sort of thing. I've also seen catalogs from companies offering novelty gifts like exploding golf balls, T-shirts and hats with funny slogans on them, silly training aids like the famous "crotch hook" (you'll learn to keep your head down—or else), and gag putters with flexible shafts that can be twisted in every direction when you get angry.

The lesson to be learned from this is that a hot market can spawn all sorts of mail-order companies, each one specializing in serving a particular niche within that market. Keep this in mind when you analyze markets for potential products.

Are the Demographics Right for the Product?

Refer back to some of the demographic trends we discussed in chapter 2. Baby boomers are a huge market, educated, affluent, slowly getting older, and ripe for all sorts of products and services. The youngest of them have generated a baby boomlet, creating a hot market for products aimed at children. The parents of boomers, the "Ikes," are wallowing in retirement with more assets than any other generation in history. And various ethnic groups are becoming attractive demographic targets.

Although these are the most obvious markets in the United States today, they're certainly not the only ones. Any group of people that share a characteristic or an interest constitutes a demographic market. Golfers are an example, as are Elvis fans. And don't forget teenagers. They'll always be attractive to merchandisers. They have a surprising amount of money and spend it freely. Mail-order music companies do a huge business with teens. Clothing businesses also do well.

IS THE MARKET LONG-TERM, OR IS THIS A FAD?

Every person who gets into the mail-order business dreams of finding that once-in-a lifetime product—their own version of the Pet Rock—that will take off and make them wealthy beyond their wildest dreams. Well, I hate to disappoint you, but it just isn't going to happen.

That's not to say you can't find a product with one-shot market appeal. You may well be able to. But what happens when that product has run its course, and its market has dried up? You're either out of business or scrambling like mad to find another product. And unless you have an absolutely uncanny sense for spotting offbeat marketing opportunities—not to mention a whole lot of luck—the chances of operating a successful mail-order business based on an endless series of one-shot wonders are absolutely nil.

Another danger of one-shot products is the temptation to try to emulate the successful ones by coming up with a similar idea. This exact thing happened about six months after the Pet Rock craze died down, when someone tried to cash in with a little item called Legal Pot. This was, in fact, a tiny saucepan, about four inches long, that was sold in a little wooden crate.

For whatever reason or reasons, Legal Pot went nowhere. It may have been the drug reference. It may have been the advertising. I've always suspected it was because the public recognized it for what it was—a blatant attempt to recreate the success of the Pet Rock. It was almost as if people were saying, "Okay, you can get us once. But twice? Forget about it." For marketing people, the failure of Legal Pot was a very interesting lesson in consumer psychology and behavior.

The lesson here is that to ensure long-term success, you must have a product or service with long-term demand. As you consider a potential product, you'll need to carefully evaluate its present marketability and its potential for future growth. What will the market be like in five years? In ten years? Are there any potential developments that could hurt sales or even make the product obsolete?

IS THE PRODUCT LIMITED SEASONALLY?

Some products have ebb and flow sales patterns based on the seasons. That doesn't mean they're bad products, but it does mean that these traits need to be factored into your decision to sell them.

If you find a product with mail-order potential but with seasonal highs and lows, you'll need to do some very careful calculations. Can you set up your business in a manner that will allow it to roll with the shifting sales patterns? You'll also have to be honest about your own abilities. Running a business with wide swings in sales volume requires discipline and the ability to carefully manage both income and expenses. Are you up to the task?

IS THE PRODUCT EASY TO SHIP?

The logistics of getting your product to your customers is an important consideration. When evaluating an item, ask yourself if it's small enough to make packing and shipping easy. Is it of reasonable weight, or so heavy that shipping might be unusually expensive? Is it sturdy enough to stand up to the not-so-gentle treatment it's likely to experience en route to the customer, or is it so fragile that it will require specially constructed shipping cartons? In the case of foods, bruising (when shipping fruit, for example) and spoilage must be taken into consideration.

CAN YOU FIND A RELIABLE SUPPLIER?

Customer service is every bit as important in mail order as it is in retail. You can't keep them waiting too long after they place an order. That means you'll need a steady, reliable supply of merchandise.

When you're considering a product, you'll need to talk to different manufacturers and suppliers of the product. Explain what you're interested in doing. Try to give them some idea of the volume you expect. Find out what sort of financial arrangement they maintain with their customers. It might not be a bad idea to check with some of their other customers to find out if they've ever had problems with the supplier.

Hopefully, you'll find more than one supplier. For one thing, it can give you some bargaining power when negotiating the price you'll pay for your products. It also means that if your regular supplier has a problem that prevents him from getting you what you need, you'll have a back-up source and won't have any interruptions in *your* business. Once you've decided on a supplier or suppliers, you can work out the fine points of your business relationship.

DOES THE PRODUCT PRESENT LEGAL RISKS?

Remember Irwin Mainway, the sleazy merchandiser played by Dan Aykroyd on *Saturday Night Live?* He had a whole bunch of hilariously menacing junk that he tried to peddle to kids, including the memorable "Bag O' Glass." This was a big bag of broken shards of glass that Irwin insisted kids would love. The only problem, as his interviewer in the skit pointed out, was that it was really, really dangerous. Only after much protest did Irwin concede she might have a point.

Well, Irwin would have a tough time in the mail-order business. The Bag O' Glass was a lawsuit waiting to happen, and that's the last thing he or anyone else in business needs. That's why you must evaluate a product for any potential dangers it may present to the user.

Many products, particularly those in which safety is an obvious factor, will often have their products approved by some sort of regulatory agency. Electrical products, for example, should be approved by the Underwriter's Laboratory. An organization called the Snell Memorial Foundation lends its name to bicycle helmets that fulfill its stringent safety requirements.

For a lot of other products, however, you're going to have to use your own common sense. For example, suppose you decide to sell a line of toys designed for toddlers and preschoolers. In this age group, a toy is likely to spend almost as much time in someone's mouth as it is being played with, so you'll need to make sure there are no small parts that could come off and get lodged in a child's throat.

Remember, we live in a society in which people file suit against each other at the drop of a hat. If you're sued, it will be expensive and time consuming, regardless of the outcome. It's important to be as safety conscious as possible.

WHAT'S NEXT?

You've chosen your product because *you* think it's a good idea. But before you get all wrapped up in putting your mail-order business together, you'll need to find out if the rest of the world agrees with you. That requires some test-marketing. In chapter 7, we'll look at how to find out if your product will fly.

❧ 7 ❧

TESTING THE MARKET

Once you've decided on the product you're going to offer, it's time to take your first tentative dip into the mail-order waters with a few market tests. This is a critical step in the process, and for one very important reason. *It helps minimize your risk!*

Risk is an inherent part of any business venture, whether it's a $1,000 start-up mail-order business run from your basement or a $10,000,000 manufacturing business that's financed to the gills. Your money and your future are on the line, so you want to be as confident as you can that your investment is going to produce the desired return. Your testing begins with finding out whether anyone is going to buy what you're selling and how much they'll pay for it.

PRICING YOUR PRODUCT

One of your goals in the testing procedure is to determine how much you can charge for the product. It's a delicate task. Obviously, there will be a minimal amount you'll need to charge to break even. Beyond that, you want to be able to charge as much as possible to maximize your profits. But you can't charge so much that you price yourself out of the market and fail to be competitive. Finding that happy medium will require a bit of work.

Your market tests will help you fine-tune your price. If you find your early tests indicating that your initial price is too high, you can lower it a bit and run another trial. If it still seems too high, lower it again and repeat the process. If you get to the point where it becomes apparent you can't charge enough to make your desired profit, you'll know it's time to look for another product.

Pricing Considerations

Pricing for mail order is entirely different than pricing for retail. If you've ever been involved in a retail business, you know that markup on a product is usually anywhere from 50 to 100 percent of its wholesale cost.

In mail order, however, there are many products being sold for three or four times their cost. In fact, many mail-order operators won't touch a product that sells for less than that. Other products are being sold at a markup closer to that of many retail stores. Here are some of the factors that will determine what you charge for your product.

Your competition

You'll need to find out what others who are offering the same product in your market area are charging. If your product is basically the same as theirs, you'll need to keep your price in the same ballpark.

The characteristics of the product

On the other hand, you may decide that your product, although widely offered, has some characteristics or qualities that make it stand out from the rest. In this case, you may be able to charge more. Your market tests will tell you whether you can charge more or not.

Your unit cost

Unit cost is a factor in pricing products in any business. If you're selling something made by someone else, unit cost is the price you pay for one unit of the product. For example, let's say you're selling an educational computer game aimed at children. The manufacturer of the game is selling you the software in lots of 100 for $1,250. That means your cost per unit is $12.50.

If you're making the product yourself, like jewelry designer Jeannie Johnston, your cost per unit will be the cost of the materials needed for one item. As we learned earlier, Jeannie likes to make several dozen of the same item at a time. Let's say she's working on a certain style of earrings, and it costs her $500 in materials to make four dozen pairs. In this case, her cost per unit would be $10.42.

Your overhead

Your overhead consists of all the other costs associated with running the business—your rent, utilities, advertising, supplies, shipping and handling costs, insurance, legal and accounting fees, employee salaries and costs, etc.

Your target sales volume

This is the number of units you expect to sell during a given period of time. Most mail-order dealers tie their price to a marketing plan that aims for either smaller sales volume with a large profit per item or larger sales volume with a smaller profit per item. Since yours will be a start-up business, I suggest you aim for smaller volume and a larger profit, at least at first. It requires far fewer resources.

Your anticipated profit

This is your bottom line, the amount you hope to make from your venture.

THE PRICING FORMULA

Once you've determined your unit cost, overhead, target sales volume, and anticipated profit, you can use these four factors in this simple formula to determine the price of your product:

$$\frac{(\text{Unit Cost} \times \text{Unit Sales}) + \text{Profit} + \text{Overhead}}{\text{Unit Sales}} = \text{Price}$$

The fixed values in this formula are the unit cost and your overhead. The variables are your unit sales and your expected profit. By juggling these two variables, you can arrive at different prices.

Let's look at the computer games again to see how you'd determine their price. You're buying the games for $12.50 each from the manufacturer. We'll assume you're anticipating a sales volume of 2,000 units and hoping to make a profit of $20,000, or $10 for each unit sold. We'll also assume you're starting small and working out of your home by yourself. Your only overhead consists of shipping materials, mailing charges, and advertising, which cost a total of $5,000. The math would be as follows:

$$\frac{(\$12.50 \times 2,000) + \$20,000 + \$5,000}{2,000} = \frac{\$50,000}{2,000} = \$25$$

So to make your desired profit, you'll need to charge $25 for each game. If your desired profit or your overhead are higher or lower, you can adjust the formula accordingly.

Adjusting Your Price

One of your goals in your testing is to determine whether or not your customers will buy your product at the price you've set. Let's say your market tests indicate that $25 is too high a price to make the games viable in the market, and that $20 is more realistic. Now you have to make some adjustments.

The only way to reach your target profit is to increase your volume. Since you know your total cost per unit is $15 (your $12.50 cost per unit plus $2.50 overhead per unit), the profit for each game you sell is now only $5 rather than $10. To figure out how many units you need to sell, you simply divide your target profit by the profit per unit.

$$\frac{\$20,000}{\$5} = 4,000$$

Suddenly the endeavor takes on a whole new complexion. At $20 per unit, which is only a 20 percent reduction in price, you'll have to *double* your sales volume to 4,000 units to make the same profit. Can you do it? Or should you look for another product to sell?

Of course, testing doesn't always reveal bad news. You might discover you can sell your product for more than you thought, say $30. In this case, you'd only need to sell 1,334 units to make your target profit. And if you reached your goal of 2,000 units sold, your profit would jump to $30,000.

DETERMINING YOUR BREAK-EVEN POINT

Your break-even point is the number of units you need to sell to cover your costs. If your sales volume exceeds this figure, you make money. If you fail to reach this figure, you lose money. If you sell exactly that number of units, you neither make nor lose money—*you break even.*

Let's look at the computer games once again. You've determined you will sell 2,000 games at $25 per unit. But there's no guarantee you'll reach that figure. What happens if you sell fewer than 2,000? At what point will you start to lose money if your sales assumptions are way off? You can figure this out with another simple formula:

$$\frac{\textbf{(Unit Cost x Unit Sales) + Overhead}}{\textbf{Unit Price}} = \textbf{Break-even point}$$

or, in this case:

$$\frac{(\$12.50 \times 2,000) + \$5,000}{\$25} = \frac{\$30,000}{\$25} = 1,200$$

So the break-even point in your computer game venture will be 1,200 units. This is the figure that will drive you day after day. The sooner you reach it, the sooner you make money.

IDENTIFYING YOUR TEST MARKET

Before you can test the market, you need to figure out who that market is. The best way to start is to buy a few mailing lists. You can buy lists from other businesses selling the same product or a similar product. You can also buy the subscription lists of magazines or other publications that your customers would be likely to read. If, like Jeannie Johnston, you've been in business for some time already, you may have compiled a list yourself.

If your product has a fairly universal appeal, meaning it might be purchased by almost anyone, regardless of age, sex, or socioeconomic status, you don't even have to go to the trouble of buying lists. You can simply create your own by using the phone book. Select a few hundred or a thousand names at random and make them your test market.

CHOOSING YOUR TESTING MEDIA

There are any number of media you can use to test the market response to your product. They run the gamut from expensive venues like television, radio, and popular national magazines to bare-bones approaches like printing and mailing out a simple do-it-yourself flyer. Your choices will be guided by the amount of money you have to spend on the process and the size of the business you're starting. (Refer to chapter 10 for a more detailed analysis of various advertising and marketing methods.)

You also need to look at where your competition advertises. We learned earlier that one of the best approaches to mail order is to sell what other people are selling. Likewise, one of the best approaches to marketing your product is to go after the customers your competitors go after by advertising in the same media.

But before you go to the expense of buying advertising space and printing flyers, there's one very direct way to get people's feedback on your product. Here's how to do it.

⑤ USE FOCUS GROUPS

The focus group is one of the most effective—and most affordable—methods of getting direct market feedback on your
product. Getting a roomful of people together and asking them
to brainstorm on the pros and cons of your product will not
only give you a good idea of its marketability but it will also
help you determine how the product might be improved.

Selecting your group

You should begin by picking a representative sample of your
target demographic market. For example, let's say you're selling
a new and improved miracle potato peeler. You know your
customers will be mostly women, they'll represent a wide range
of ages, and they'll include all ethnic and socioeconomic
groups. When you sit down with your focus group, you'd better
be looking at a roomful of women of all ages, colors, and
incomes.

On the other hand, suppose you're selling a do-it-yourself
pinstriping kit for automobiles. In this case, your demographic
target is largely young men ages eighteen to thirty, representing
all ethnic groups, and leaning toward the middle and lower-
middle socioeconomic classes (I think it's safe to assume the
more affluent young car owners will pay someone to do their
pinstriping for them). Again, your focus group should reflect
these demographic characteristics.

Some marketing books suggest using friends or family members for your focus group. I strongly disagree, and for a very
good reason. You need to have as unbiased an audience as
possible when seeking feedback on your product, and you're
not going to get unbiased answers from people who know you.
They're going to be either overly critical out of concern for
your well-being or overly positive because they're afraid of
hurting your feelings.

Consider your mom, for example. Do you really think your
mom is going to give you a straight answer? If she's like mine,
she'll sit there beaming with pride, thinking your idea is just

wonderful. It's only after your business goes down in flames that she'll reluctantly admit there might have been a problem.

Hand out your product

Make sure you bring plenty of samples of your product to the meeting for people to try. And, of course, let them keep the samples as a show of your appreciation for their time. If using the product at the meeting is impractical, as might be the case with the pinstriping kit, distribute it beforehand so your group will have a chance to try it before they meet. And don't forget refreshments.

If you have a product with fairly universal appeal, you might consider setting up a small table at a mall or some other location with a lot of pedestrian traffic. The idea is to get as much consumer response as possible. Put up a sign offering free samples of your product. Let people try out the product and talk to them to get some feedback. Maybe have them fill out a questionnaire, but one that's short enough to do right on the spot in just a minute or two.

One bit of advice: Often you'll see people handing out questionnaires with postage-paid return envelopes so the questionnaires can be filled out later and mailed in. Don't waste your money. Once they're out of your sight, most people are going to forget all about you. Your questionnaire—and your expensive return envelope—are just going to end up in the trash.

What should you ask?

You've gathered your group together for a reason, so you need to know beforehand exactly what you want them to tell you. Here are some of the questions you should ask.

- How often do you buy this type of product?
- How much do you usually pay for this type of product?
- Where do you usually purchase this type of product?
- Do you buy whatever you happen to run across, or do you stick to a particular product brand or source?

- Would you be comfortable purchasing this type of product via mail order, or would you prefer to purchase it in person?
- Does my product meet your expectations for quality and performance?
- Is my product reasonably priced?
- Would you continue to purchase my product?
- How can my product be improved?

Pay careful attention to their answers. When people know they're being asked for an honest opinion, they usually won't hesitate to give you one. If they tell you your product is lousy, or they don't like the idea of buying it by mail order, find out why. If they think it's too expensive or could be improved, make some adjustments. You also want to find out if they think it's a real bargain for the money. That means you might be able to charge more.

It's usually not a bad idea to conduct a number of focus groups spread out within the geographic area in which you'll be doing business. Your ability to do this may be limited by your finances, however.

Ⓢ PREPARE YOUR OWN MAILING

This is probably the easiest and cheapest method of testing your product. You can use your computer (you've purchased a computer by this point, right?) to create a simple flyer. Then you can use your printer (you've purchased one of these, too, I assume) to print out however many copies you think you'll need.

This approach will give you about as bare-bones a flyer as you would want—a single-page, 8½-by-11-inch sheet of paper, printed in black, folded to letter size, and ready to be mailed. It'll certainly be inexpensive and simple. The problem is, depending on what you're selling, it might be a little *too* spartan.

In mail order—as in all businesses—image is extremely important. For this reason, you need to tailor your advertising to your product. For example, if you're selling the new and improved miracle potato peeler, a simple computer-generated flyer is probably more than adequate. But if you're selling something with a little more class, you might want to get a bit fancier.

In this case, you could work with a graphic designer to help you develop a more professional-looking flyer. It could have another color in addition to black and maybe even include a photograph of the product. The designer can also give you advice on various types of paper and different methods of printing. Although going this route will cost a bit more, it still won't break the bank. If you're trying to create a certain image for your product, it's money well spent.

When you do your own mailing, you'll need to check with the post office to learn about bulk mail regulations and how your flyer must be folded and addressed. We'll discuss mailing regulations in chapter 12.

⑤ TRY THE CLASSIFIEDS

The classified ads in the back of magazines and newspapers are the cheapest form of print advertising you can buy, and therefore the perfect place for a fledgling mail-order business to advertise its wares. You can usually purchase a three- or four-line ad for $10 to $20 a week in most newspapers, and for about the same amount per issue in many magazines. The classifieds are small and fairly obscure, but you'd be surprised at the number of people who read them faithfully every day.

Because classifieds are bunched together and printed in small type, it's important to get your ad noticed. The best way is to come up with a short sentence at the beginning of the ad that can be printed in bold type. For example, if you were running an ad for the computer game, you might word your ad like this:

GIVE YOUR CHILD A HEAD START IN READING! Our computer game is a fun way for your child to learn the alphabet, letter sounds, and the basics of reading. Send check or money order for $25

to CompuKid, Dept. A, P.O. Box 100, Anytown, N.Y. 11111. Specify
Mac or PC. Allow 4 weeks for delivery.

By bolding the first sentence, you've maximized your chances
of getting the readers' attention. And by making it clear that
you're selling a product that will help children, you can be sure
than anyone with a small child will read the entire ad. People
are anxious to give their children as much of a head start in
life as they can. Your first sentence takes advantage of this fact.

TRY A DISPLAY AD

If you feel like making a bit more of an investment, you can
purchase a larger "display" ad to run in a magazine or newspaper. Display ads can be anywhere from a column in width and
an inch in height to the size of a full page, with prices increasing with size.

In this case, you'll need to consider the graphic design of the
ad as well as the ad copy. If you're not comfortable doing your
own graphics work, the art departments of many newspapers and
magazines will help you with a design. You might also be able
to find a freelance graphic designer who can provide you with a
design for relatively little money. And if you're near a college or
university, don't overlook the availability of students. Many superb
graphic design students will work with you for next to nothing. It
brings them a little money and it gives them some professional
experience they can add to their portfolio.

Of course, the downside to this tactic is the added expense.
The larger the ad, and the more prominent its location, the more
it will cost. But that doesn't mean that this kind of advertising
should be avoided if you're starting your business on the cheap.
Advertising costs are usually tied to the circulation of the publication, so many small newspapers and magazines may be quite
affordable. It just takes a phone call to find out.

COMPARING RESPONSE RATES

One of the things testing will tell you, in addition to whether
your product is marketable and priced correctly, is which media

give you the best response rates. Once you've sent out flyers
and run ads in various publications, and orders begin to come
in, you can compare response rates by keeping track of which
orders were generated by which media.

Key your ads

If you're going to compare the response rates, you need to be
able to tell which ads generated which orders. To do that you
need to put an identifying "key" in your address.

   As an example, you'll notice that the address in the classified
ad for the kid's educational computer software includes a
"Dept. A." That's the key that will let you know that a particular order was in response to a particular ad you placed in a
particular publication. When you run the ad, or a different ad,
in a second publication, you can use Dept. B. For a third ad or
a third publication, use Dept. C. You get the picture.

   Depending on how complex you get with your testing, you
may need a whole variety of keys in your address. Let's say
you're trying out three different ads, and you're running each
ad in four different publications. That would mean you'd need
twelve different keys. However you choose to organize them is
up to you. Just make sure you key them correctly, or the information you gather will be completely erroneous. And if you act
on that information, you could lose a great deal of money.

Tabulating the results

Let's say you've tried out five different media for the initial
test of your computer game. The first is a mailer you designed
and printed yourself and sent out to 1,000 families in the area
with three- to five-year-olds. You can usually get the names
and addresses of these people by obtaining the student/parent
directories of nursery schools and elementary schools. Since the
directories are organized by grade, you can determine which
families have children in the proper age range. The printing and
postal costs for the mailing total $250.

   For the second test you sent out another 1,000 mailers to the
names on a mailing list you purchased from a local toy store

for $100. The cost of the list, combined with the $250 cost for printing and mailing the 1,000 mailers, brought the total cost of this test to $350.

The third and fourth tests were ads in two different newspapers. The first was a classified ad you ran for a week in the large daily paper that covers your town and the surrounding communities. The second was a small display ad run once in a weekly "freebie" newspaper that people pick up in local businesses, the library, and other locations. Your fifth test was the same display ad you ran in the newspaper. Only this one was run in a monthly, nationally distributed parenting magazine with a circulation of 350,000.

At the end of the testing period, you can create a chart to compare the responses you received from each ad. Comparing the number of responses to the circulation of the various media will tell you what percentage of recipients responded. You can also divide the cost of each ad by the number of responses to determine the cost per response.

Media	Circulation	Cost	Responses	% Resp	Cost Per Resp
Mailer #1	1,000	$250	87	8.7	$2.87
Mailer #2	1,000	$350	20	2.0	$17.50
News Clsfd	57,000	$40	68	.12	$.59
News Display	12,000	$75	37	.31	$2.03
Mag Display	350,000	$475	385	.11	$1.23

NOTE: These figures are purely hypothetical and in no way intended to indicate the response to, or effectiveness of, various forms of advertising. Customer response to advertising is influenced by many factors and will vary widely depending on these factors. These examples are intended only to illustrate the concept of comparing customer response.

Analyzing the results

Once you've totaled your figures, you should notice some interesting things. First, you'll see that your two direct mailings had by far the highest response rates. You might get pretty excited by that fact—until you analyze the cost per response. They, too, were much higher than those of your other tests.

The reasons for these figures are simple. Consider your first mailing. It was unquestionably the most accurately targeted. Because every family that received the mailer had a child or children in your target age range, each was a potential customer. So it's no surprise that the response rate was as high as it was. And the response to your second mailing was still much higher than the response to the three ads, in spite of the fact that not all the customers of a toy store will have children in the three-to-five-year age range.

But when you look at the cost per response for your mailers, you see that the first was fairly high and the second right through the roof. This is because, compared to other forms of advertising, mailers are a fairly expensive form of customer contact, despite their simplicity. At $250 per 1,000 flyers, your first mailing cost you a quarter for each household you contacted. The second mailing, at $350, cost 35 cents per contact.

The newspaper classified ad, on the other hand, proved to be the cheapest form of advertising. Even though the response rate was minuscule, barely a tenth of a percent, the cost of each response was a fraction of your mailer responses. Classifieds allow you to get your ad in front of tens of thousands of people for next to nothing. In the case of your local daily, you were able to get your ad into fourteen households for each penny you spent. That's pretty good exposure for very little money.

Comparing profitability

Testing response rates will help you weed out those media that aren't worth using. In the preceding example, only one—the mailer using the toy store's mailing list—proved completely ineffective. It generated only twenty sales, and each one cost you $17.50 in advertising overhead. When your product is selling for only $25.00, making a profit is out of the question.

Your other mailer, at a cost of $2.87 per sale, was marginal in effectiveness. We'd already seen that your target overhead to earn your desired profit of $10.00 per unit sold was $2.50 per unit. The $2.87 per unit advertising cost, combined with the materials and shipping costs that make up the rest of your overhead, would reduce that profit considerably. Still, you might decide to keep using it. You'd also probably consider using the newspaper display ad. With a cost per unit of $2.03, it brings you even closer to your desired overhead and profit.

The newspaper classified, on the other hand, worked marvelously, costing you just 59 cents for each unit sold. This allows you to keep your overhead per unit well below $2.50. And the magazine classified, although nowhere near as effective as the newspaper ad, still had a low enough cost per response to keep your overhead within your target figure.

Let's compare the profitability of the five strategies. To the advertising cost for each order, we'll add $1.25 for materials and shipping to make up the entire overhead cost. Then we'll look at total profit and profit per unit sold.

Mailer #1

Generated 87 sales @ $25.00	$2,175.00
Less cost ($12.50/unit)	1,087.50
	1,087.50
Less overhead ($4.12/unit)	358.44
Profit	$729.06
Profit per unit sold	$8.38

Mailer #2

Generated 20 sales @ $25.00	$500.00
Less cost ($12.50/unit)	250.00
	250.00
Less overhead ($18.75/unit)	375.00
Profit	($125.00)
Profit per unit sold	($6.25)

Newspaper Classified Ad

Generated 68 sales @ $25.00	$1,700.00
Less cost ($12.50/unit)	850.00
	850.00
Less overhead ($1.84/unit)	125.12
Profit	$724.88
Profit per unit sold	$10.66

Newspaper Display Ad

Generated 37 sales @ $25.00	$925.00
Less cost ($12.50/unit)	462.50
	462.50
Less overhead ($3.28/unit)	121.36
Profit	$341.14
Profit per unit sold	$9.22

Magazine Display Ad

Generated 385 sales @ $25.00	$9,625.00
Less cost ($12.50/unit)	4,812.50
	4,812.50
Less overhead ($2.48/unit)	954.80
Profit	$3,857.70
Profit per unit sold	$10.02

Of the five strategies, the newspaper classified was the best, allowing you to earn 66 cents more than your target profit per unit. And the magazine display ad, although less profitable, still kept you a couple of pennies above the $10.00 profit per sale mark. The newspaper display ad and the first mailer, although earning you below your target profit, were close enough to merit consideration. But look at the second mailer. It failed to generate enough orders to break even, and you lost $125.00 for your efforts. So much for *that* mailing list.

You can use this method to compare not just advertising costs. It's also useful in comparing profits from selling your product at different prices and with various overhead costs.

YOUR TESTING WILL BE ONGOING

One of the facts of life in the mail-order business is that all the factors in the business—sales volume, product prices, advertising strategies and responses, sales patterns—must be constantly monitored to make sure your business stays pointed in the right direction. This means that testing will be an ongoing part of the process.

Every time you advertise your product, whether it's in a display ad, a classified ad, or a mailer, everything is being tested—the price of the product, the ad copy, the publication in which the ad is placed, the design of the ad, the illustrations, the placement of the ad in the publication, and (in the case of a mailer) the mailing list. For example, an ad that has performed admirably for three or four years may suddenly prove to be ineffective. Or a publication that has always provided great response may begin to produce fewer orders.

Sometimes, you might find your customer response falling off across the board. All your ads suddenly stop performing as well as they have in the past. In this case, it's probably either that the price of your product has gone out of line or the product is losing viability in the market.

As you test different media, you'll discover a variety of advertising opportunities. For instance, the 30,000 circulation daily newspaper in my town has a monthly "Kids' Corner" advertising section in its Saturday edition. This section is anywhere from a quarter to a half page, and it's filled with ads for products and services aimed at children. You wouldn't know for sure until you tested it, but placing your software ad in this section would certainly seem like a strategy that would generate a lot of sales. We also have a weekly freebie with a lower circulation. It, too, has periodic kids' sections that would no doubt be fruitful places to run such an ad.

WHAT'S NEXT?

Testing your product is critical to determining whether or not it will successfully support your mail-order business. Testing properly takes time and should be done thoroughly and thought-fully. Our discussion introduced you to some of the basics of advertising. We'll look at advertising more thoroughly in chap-ter 10.

During the testing process, you're in business, but not yet 100 percent. Once you've decided your product is a good one, however, it'll be time to get your business operating in full swing. In chapter 8 we'll look at how to set up your business.

⤜ 8 ⤛

SETTING UP YOUR BUSINESS

Choosing a product will be just the first task in getting your mail-order business up and running. You'll still need to get legal and accounting advice, decide where to locate the business, select a business structure, get the proper equipment and supplies, and fill out a lot of forms. But before you do all of that, you'll need to figure out what you're going to call your new venture.

CHOOSING A NAME

At first glance, this might seem like a task that won't require much effort. But once you start thinking about it, you'll realize just how important a name is to a business. Then you'll be amazed at how much time you spend agonizing over your decision.

The reason is simple. Your business name is an important piece of advertising. It's almost always the first thing a customer comes in contact with, so it needs to stand out from the other advertising that people are deluged with every day. It should accurately reflect what you sell, and it should project the kind of image you want to convey. It needs to grab your customers' attention, be easy for them to remember, and sound a bit exciting and contemporary.

KEEP IT SIMPLE

A good business name is one that says as much about you as possible in as few words as possible. So your real challenge will be to cram a lot of information about the business into just a word or two.

Let's look at your hypothetical software business again and bounce around a few names. Unfortunately, Microsoft is already taken, so maybe you should just name it after yourself and call it Bob's Software or Sue's Software. It's certainly simple enough. But it's also pretty boring. Plus it doesn't give any indication that you're selling a product designed for kids.

On the other hand, how about CompuKid, the name we used in the sample ad? It's not too bad. It tells the customer you're selling a computer product aimed at kids. It also has a nice alliterative ring to it, so it'll be easy for people to remember. Other good choices might be TeachWare or KidWare. The important thing is to make sure the name reflects your product and gets noticed.

THINK LONG TERM

You'll need to have some foresight in choosing a name so that it's not limiting over the long term. CompuKid certainly works great for your business as it stands now, but it also limits you to selling software aimed at children. If you think you might eventually want to expand your product line to include software for all age groups, you need to select a name that will be all-inclusive.

GETTING IDEAS

The best way to come up with a name for your business is to sit down with a pad and pencil and start brainstorming. Make a list of all the positive things you can think of about your product. Make another list of words related to the product and your target audience. Is there anything special about your location that might be incorporated into your name? Does the product have any unusual characteristics that you might use?

Don't hesitate to involve your spouse or your friends and relatives, either. Getting a group of people together can be especially productive. People start to bounce ideas off one another, and some real creativity can be generated. Also, don't forget a thesaurus and a dictionary.

HOW ABOUT AN ADDRESS?

This is another important decision. Do you use the actual street address of your home or office, or should you rent a post office box? There are advantages and disadvantages to each.

A post office box address will keep your ads shorter and therefore less expensive. It's very convenient if you move to a new home or change offices. And the cost of the box is a business expense and can be deducted from your business income. But a post office box address is also somewhat impersonal and doesn't always elicit a lot of trust in customers. It also means a trip to the post office at least once a day to pick up your mail.

Using your actual address might make your business seem a little more user-friendly. It also means your mail arrives at your door every day, saving you a trip to the post office to pick it up. This is an especially important consideration if you live a fairly long distance from the post office. On the downside, though, using your real address means that your customers know where you live, if you operate your business from home. This could have some undesirable effects on your privacy.

REGISTERING YOUR NAME

In most counties, businesses are required to register their names with the county clerk's office. The filing fee will vary from county to county and must usually be paid within thirty days of opening for business. You'll probably have to enter a public notice in your local paper of your intent to do business under that name. You should also check the records to see if anyone else in the area is already conducting business under the name you've chosen.

If you're starting a business that will be operating in a larger region or even nationally, you'll want to have your attorney conduct a name clearance investigation.

Choosing Your Visual Image

After you've selected your name, you should give some thought to your visual identity. At the very least, you'll probably want to have a logo designed. A logo is the visual representation of your business and will appear on your letterhead, business cards, invoices, advertising, and all other material. It can be a stylized version of a name, such as the famous Coca-Cola logo that's recognized worldwide, or an identifying graphic like the Mercedes-Benz medallion.

If you have some artistic talent and want to design your own logo, this is where you can have some fun with your computer. Look at the logos of other companies to get ideas of fonts (typefaces) you find attractive. Then experiment with the different fonts in your word processing program to create your own logo. Experiment with different type sizes, too. If you don't have confidence in your own abilities, you can hire a good graphic designer, who can come up with a simple logo for a nominal fee. Desktop publishing businesses will also work with you to help you design a logo.

Stationery and Business Cards

After you've selected a logo, you'll need to have business cards and stationery printed. These should include the name and address of your business, your phone number, fax number, and E-mail address. Your business card should also have your name on it.

Visit a few print shops to get some idea of prices. And keep in mind that in printing, the major expense for the printer is setting up the job prior to the actual print run. For this reason, the more copies of something you have printed, the cheaper the cost per copy. So you might as well have a lot done at one time. It will save you money over the long haul.

Be extra sure to have a lot of business cards printed. They're inexpensive and a great form of advertising. Always carry them with you, and hand them out to everyone you meet.

HOME OR OFFICE?

As we've already learned, in the interest of saving money you'll want to operate at home unless it's absolutely impossible. And the only things that would make it impossible are selling a product that demands a lot of space or local laws that prohibit the operation of home-based businesses. That brings us to the first step in the process.

CHECK THE ZONING LAWS

Home-based businesses are growing by leaps and bounds these days. But in many communities, their growth is being hampered by antiquated zoning laws. For this reason, it's important that you find out what the zoning regulations are in your community before you begin to set up shop. If you don't, you may find yourself tangled up in a legal hassle down the road that could put you out of business.

The problem is that most of these zoning laws were put into place decades ago to protect residential neighborhoods from the noise, smoke, and traffic generated by factories. They were enacted during the industrialization of America, and there's no question they were appropriate for the times. The problem is that many communities have failed to recognize the radical shifts in the American workforce. We've moved to a service-oriented, high-tech, small business economy. But still in place are many zoning laws that were designed to keep out fire-belching factories, which no longer exist.

The problem is so absurd that even the quietest, most innocuous business people, such as accountants and freelance writers, are technically violating the law in many communities by working at home. Granted, there's little chance they'll get caught unless they get one of the neighbors angry at them. But other home business operators have run into problems when a sign on their lawn or a steady parade of clients tipped off authorities about their business.

Property is usually zoned in one of four categories: residential, commercial, industrial, or agricultural. It's doubtful you live in an area zoned for industry, and if you live in an agricultural or commercial area, you'll probably have no problem. But if you live in a residential area, you'll need to do further research to find out what kinds of businesses are allowed and whether there are any restrictions that apply to those businesses. There's an excellent chance there will be; nine out of ten communities put some restrictions on home businesses. Typically, there are rules about signage, client parking, employees, storage, and the hours you can be open for business.

If you're lucky, you won't have too many problems. You won't have people visiting your business, so you won't have to worry about parking or generating a lot of traffic. You won't really need a sign. And you won't be generating a lot of noise. The only thing that will really distinguish you from your neighbors is the inordinate amount of mail you send and receive. The only person who might *really* get upset with you is the mailman.

Check Your Lease

If you rent your home or are a member of a condominium or community association, you'll need to make sure there are no clauses in your lease or association agreement forbidding the operation of a business on the premises. It's understandable why the clause might be in there. If you're a renter, your landlord will certainly want to make sure there's nothing going on that could damage the property or annoy the neighbors. And if you're a member of a community association, the other residents want to make sure their peace and quiet will be undisturbed.

If you do find a conflict, just realize that all is not lost. Rules are made to be broken, and if you can convince the landlord or your community association that your business will not cause a problem, you might be able to swing them to your side.

Advantages of the Home-Based Business

As a home-based business owner, you'll be joining millions of other people who have discovered the convenience of working at home. Michael Antoniak, whose *How to Start a Home Business* is another book in The 21st Century Entrepreneur series, calls these people "homies." It's estimated that there are as many as 20 million of them.

Some homies are operating their own businesses. Others are employees of corporations that have come to realize the cost-effectiveness of having their employees work at home. All are enjoying the many pleasures that come with working at home:

- It saves money. Not paying rent and utilities removes a great deal of the overhead from your business. It can reduce the capital you'll need for start-up by as much as 75 percent.

- It gives you complete autonomy over everything in the business, from the hours you work to the way the place is laid out to how you choose to dress for work each day. And don't underestimate the money you can save by eliminating the need for an office wardrobe.

- It eliminates commuting, saving you time and money and protecting the environment from unnecessary air pollution.

- You know how people say a place has all the comforts of home? Well, your workplace will have exactly that.

- You can claim a portion of your rent or mortgage as a business expense on your taxes.

- It removes a great deal of risk from the process. If the business doesn't pan out, you can just turn your office back into an extra bedroom.

DISADVANTAGES OF THE HOME-BASED BUSINESS

Like anything else, a home-based business does have some downsides. Many homies say the biggest difficulty is establishing good work habits. I'm certainly one of them. I'll frequently find myself wandering around the house when I work at home. I'll usually end up in the kitchen to grab a snack (that's another problem with working at home—you might eat too much) and end up washing the dishes or cleaning out the refrigerator. Sometimes I get wrapped up in a game of computer golf. I've been known to take the dogs on absurdly long walks. I've also been known to fall sound asleep in front of my computer.

I have a good friend, also a writer, whose big problem is the television. He kept one in his home office until the Gulf War, which he watched practically from start to finish on CNN. He finally removed it and was doing okay until the O. J. Simpson trial, which he started watching on the television in his family room. Finally, his wife had a lock put on the door to the room and took the key to work with her each day.

"Just say no to O. J.," she told him.

Distractions like food and television are just two of the disadvantages of working at home. Here are some others:

- Loneliness. Many homies go the entire day without interacting with another person. Some love it. But those who don't usually list it as their biggest complaint.

- Your business life can be disrupted. If your family is home during the day, it can be very distracting. Another problem is that, because the office is just a few steps away, a lot of homies tend to become workaholics, and this can cause a great deal of domestic stress.

- Lack of a support system. When you work in an office, you can usually get help from coworkers if it's needed. When you're by yourself, all the responsibilities fall on your shoulders.

- Your space may be limited. Although most people can generally find *some* space in their home to use as an office or workplace, it's not always as big or as comfortable as they'd like.

- Customers may find it uncomfortable or inconvenient to come to your home, particularly if you live far out of town or in a neighborhood where parking is difficult to find.

SETTING UP YOUR HOME OFFICE

One of the great things about operating a mail-order business out of your home is the fact that your customers won't be coming to your place of business. That means you don't have to worry about appearances and can set up your work space exactly as you want.

Would you like to have a basketball hoop on the wall? No problem. Have you always wanted to hang your Three Stooges poster in the office? Knock yourself out. How about a reclining chair in the corner? It's your choice.

As you set things up, keep in mind that the ideal home office has several characteristics:

- It has ample room for your basic equipment plus any other tools or materials needed for your business.

- It's far enough removed from the rest of your home to protect you from the bustle and noise of your family and ensure your privacy.

- It's used exclusively for your business and doesn't have a secondary function as a storage room, a playroom for the kids, or a hobby room for your spouse.

- It has its own door, preferably one that opens to the outside.

- It provides you with ample room for all your day-to-day activities as well as for storage and record keeping.

- It's well lit, well ventilated, and has a window that opens.

Perhaps the most important of these characteristics is the second. Your privacy is critical to your happiness and satisfaction. If you don't feel adequately separated from the noise and activity in the rest of the house, you'll find it extremely difficult to give your full attention to the matters at hand. Constant interruptions from children or your spouse will drive you nuts.

It's also important that the room function solely as your office. It shouldn't be an after-hours playroom for the kids or a family room. Running a business requires organization, and if you have people playing on your computer, rearranging your files, and shuffling through your papers, you'll quickly become quite ˎ*dis*organized.

EQUIPMENT AND SUPPLIES

No matter how frugal you intend to be in starting your mail-order business, there are certain things that are absolutely necessary.

We'll begin by looking at the electronic equipment you'll need. Collectively, this equipment will probably be your major investment. You don't need to buy the most expensive stuff on the market. But don't scrimp, either. Remember, this will be your link to your customers and your suppliers. You want to make sure you have a reliable system in place.

TELEPHONE

We'll begin with the obvious. You'll need a phone, and one that's dedicated solely to your business and not shared with the rest of the family. Have a new line installed, and make sure it runs only to your office. The last thing you need is your three-year-old serving as your receptionist.

Depending on your needs, you can select from a variety of phone options. Many models today allow you to load a dozen or more numbers into the phone's memory, enabling you to dial frequently called numbers with the push of a button. If you anticipate juggling a lot of calls at one time, you may need a hold button. Telephone headsets that allow you to keep both hands free to take notes or accomplish other tasks are also available. Portable phones are very convenient, although you run the risk of other people accidentally overhearing your conversations.

The phone company will also offer options you may want to consider. Call waiting is usually a valuable and inexpensive investment. Other custom calling features include caller ID (to let you know who's calling), call forwarding, conference calling for business meetings held over the phone, and voice mail messaging.

Your phone connection will channel much more than just voice communication into your office. It also will connect your fax machine and, if you choose to have one, the modem for your computer. In fact, you may find that one line is not enough and that you need to have a separate line for each piece of equipment. You can also buy a switcher that will automatically route each incoming call to the phone, the fax, or the computer.

Should you get a toll-free number?

No. Not at first, anyway. An 800 number is expensive. Although it's certainly a nice service for your customers, it's a cost you can do without for a while. As the business grows, you might want to consider having one installed.

ANSWERING MACHINE

This is a must. No business, no matter how small, can afford poor customer relations, particularly if you accept phone orders. And there's nothing more aggravating to a customer than calling a business and not getting an answer, so an answering machine is fairly inexpensive insurance against unhappy customers. You can buy one for less than $100. Keep your message short and businesslike, remember to check your messages every time you return to the office, and return calls as soon as possible.

FAX MACHINE

As fax machines have come down in price, they've become an invaluable tool for home businesses. For your purposes, they're an excellent device for receiving orders from customers and sending orders for merchandise and supplies to your own vendors.

Fax machines come with a wide variety of features and in a wide variety of prices. Basic features include line in/line out, an automatic paper cutter, automatic transmission, and a multipage document feeder. Beyond that, you'll need to determine what special features you'll need. One feature that's useful when the receiving machine is busy is the automatic call back. This allows you to go about your business while your machine automatically redials the receiving machine until it gets through. When it does, it feeds your document through the scanner and sends it on its way. Some machines have memory features that allow you to scan a document and have it sent later, or have it resent over and over until it's received.

Before buying a fax machine, check out its image quality by sending a few test documents. Most faxes still use thermal paper, which tends to fade and wrinkle over time. There are faxes available that use plain paper, but they're still quite pricey. You can also buy machines that function as a fax, a copier, and a printer for your computer, but again, they may be priced out of your reach. Don't feel too covetous of them. Generally they are barely adequate and quite slow as printers and copiers.

If you use a computer, you might want to buy a fax/modem. This will allow you to send faxes of documents right from your computer, eliminating the need for hard copy. Be aware, however, that computers receive faxes as graphic documents, not text documents. That means they take up a lot of hard disk space and can't be edited.

COMPUTER

The computer has so revolutionized the way we live and work that no business—or home, for that matter—should be without one. As I pointed out in chapter 4, your computer will organize and store all your financial records, keep track of your inventory, and store your mailing lists. You'll use it to design flyers, prepare your correspondence, send and receive electronic messages, and for countless other things.

If you intend to do business on the Internet, your computer will become even more critical. It will serve as your electronic catalog, a ''site'' on the Internet that people will visit to peruse your products or learn about your service. Your computer will receive and store your customers' electronic orders. And it will allow you, if necessary, to communicate with them.

What to Buy

Here's some good news. Computer technology is advancing by leaps and bounds while prices basically stay the same. To give you some idea of just how much more you get for your money each passing year, consider this:

In the last five years, my family has purchased three computers, each in the neighborhood of $2,000. The first one, a Macintosh LC, was a relatively slow machine with 4 megabytes of RAM, 40 megabytes of hard disk space (jumped up from 20 megabytes by the dealer), and a 12-inch color monitor.

About two years ago, figuring my daughter would take the LC to college, I bought a Mac Performa 636CD. It was like going from a Plymouth Reliant to a Porsche! It has a built-in CD-ROM, 8 megs of RAM, 250 megs of hard disk space, a 14-inch color monitor, a ton of software, and a few CDs. Then last year, my wife, who's also a writer, began doing a lot of work at home, and we realized we each needed our own machine. So we bought her a Performa just like mine—except hers is even faster and has *500* megs of hard disk space (and I want it). Then just the other day, I saw her machine on sale for about $1,700! I couldn't believe it!

When you consider a computer, think of it in terms of a system. The basic package will include a central processing unit (CPU) with an internal hard disk, a monitor, and a keyboard. Depending on your needs, you might add any of the following: a printer, modem, fax/modem, CD-ROM drive, external hard drive, and scanner.

You can also choose between a desktop system, a portable computer that folds up to the size of a small briefcase, or a "dockable" system designed to function in both environments.

When you buy a computer, you'll need to choose between a Macintosh and a PC. Macs are made by Apple Computer and have their own very distinctive operating system. PC is a generic term that refers to just about all other computers (including IBM, the company that first marketed the personal computer, or PC) because they all *share* a common operating system. Because of the differences in the two systems, software that runs on a Mac won't run on a PC, and vice versa. There have been discussions on the adoption of a universal operating system, but the industry doesn't seem to be getting anywhere close to actually doing it.

If you've used a computer before, your best move is to buy the system you're familiar with. If you're new to the computer game, for my money Macs are infinitely easier and more fun to use. Their only drawback is that, because they represent only about 10 percent of the computer market, there's less software for them than for PCs. Having said that, however, I'll also point out that I've been more than happy with the selection that does exist.

Whatever you buy, these are the basic features you want: a system with the fastest processor (the faster the processor, the faster the computer operates), and a system with at least 8 megabytes of RAM and 500 megabytes of hard disk space.

RAM stands for random access memory, the portion of the computer's memory that is devoted to letting you work on documents and projects. Hard disk space is the amount of memory devoted to the storage of software, documents, and projects. To put it in three-dimensional terms, think of RAM as the amount of room you have on the top of your desk to work on things and hard disk space as the amount of storage space you have in your desk and filing cabinets.

You'll also need a system that's expandable. Another useful item is a CD-ROM (compact disc-read only memory) unit. These are becoming standard parts of most computers. If yours doesn't have a built-in CD-ROM, you can buy a freestanding unit that will connect to your CPU. Compact discs hold an incredible amount of data in text, audio, and graphic form. At the moment, they can only be used to store data. As soon as the technology to record data on them becomes cheap enough, and that day isn't too far off, they'll become even more useful.

To gain access to the Internet or one of the commercial on-line services, you'll need a modem. This device attaches your computer to the telephone lines, which are used for the transmission of electronic data. An even wiser purchase might be a fax/modem, which lets you send and receive documents directly from and to your computer. The speed at which this is accomplished is called the baud rate, and the higher the number, the faster it will transfer data. The technology has been steadily advancing; as this book is being written, 28,800 is the fastest modem available.

You should also consider ergonomics when buying your machine. Is the monitor clear and bright? Is the keyboard comfortable to use? Does the mouse work easily and track well?

Peripherals

Peripherals are additional pieces of hardware you can add to your system to meet your needs. The most common is a printer. Do you need one? You bet you do. Otherwise, you'll be unable to print out invoices, letters, order forms, spreadsheets, and all the other documents you'll create on your machine.

The simplest and cheapest printers produce a dot matrix document. Mid-priced printers use a thermal ink jet technology, and the best printers are laser printers. When you're comparing different printers, consider the speed with which they print, the visual quality of the documents, and the expense of the ink or toner cartridges. Also, make sure the documents don't smear.

As with computers, printer technology is continually improving. My recommendation is a thermal ink jet printer, which you can buy for less than $300. I've been using one for several years and have been more than happy with it. It produces quality documents, and it's relatively fast.

Other peripherals include a scanner, which can scan images to be stored on your hard disk. You can also buy an external hard drive to add additional memory to your system. These are expensive, however, and certainly not necessary to run your business.

The Basic Software

Computers are great, but they're pretty useless without software. It's kind of like owning a Corvette but not having any gas to put in it. You can sit there and admire it, but that's about it.

Software is what makes the computer do the things you want it to do. Just as there are basic tools that should be found in every office, there are basic software programs that should be included in every business computer. Depending on your needs, you can augment them with additional programs.

For your start-up mail-order business, your two biggest needs will be a word-processing program for correspondence and a basic financial management program to keep track of your financial information. A database program will also be useful for keeping records of customers, projects, and other information.

There are many programs on the market that can accomplish these tasks. Some—Claris Works comes to mind because it came preloaded on my Mac—include these types of programs plus several others "bundled" in a single package. Like Apple, many computer manufacturers are including this type of software for free as a marketing tool; chances are the computer you buy will already have the basic software you'll need.

Once you have the basics, you can augment them with other programs that serve your needs. And, if I may make a suggestion, you should get yourself a few games. All work and no play makes for a very dull day, indeed.

OFFICE FURNISHINGS

We discussed this in chapter 4. This is *not* where you want to spend your money, so I suggest you operate by my favorite business credo: *Cheap is good. Free is better!*

Yes, you'll need a desk and a couple of chairs. No, you shouldn't run out and spend a lot of money on them. If you can't find what you need around the house, visit a swap meet or go to a secondhand store. You might even be able to find something that fills your needs sitting out by the curb on trash day. This is America, remember? People throw out perfectly good stuff all the time.

Your computer will help cut down on paperwork, but it won't eliminate it altogether, so you might find a filing cabinet useful. An extra table is useful for your printer and other equipment. And don't forget that tried and true office staple, the in/out basket. Again, this is stuff you can find for just a few bucks if you scrounge around a bit.

OFFICE SUPPLIES

You should start with the basics and fill in as needs present themselves. Get some pens and pencils, a pencil sharpener (hand-crank only, of course. Remember, electricity costs money), file folders, a stapler, paper clips, a few pads of note-paper, computer paper, some transparent tape, and an extra ink cartridge or toner cartridge for the computer. And don't forget those other office staples—''white-out'' and sticky notes.

INSURANCE

All businesses need insurance. The type and amount are dictated by the size of the business and the value of the assets it needs to protect. Your insurance agent will be able to provide the coverage that meets your needs.

At the outset of your mail-order business, your biggest investment will probably be your electronic equipment. Make sure everything—your computer, phones, and all other equipment—is covered by your homeowner's policy. Chances are it is, but if it's not, take the proper steps to arrange coverage. You can purchase computer insurance, to cover both the main system and peripherals, as a separate policy.

One way to protect your electronic equipment against damage from power surges is to invest in a surge protector. It's an inexpensive item that can save you hundreds or even thousands of dollars in repairs and incalculable mental anguish. If there should be a surge of power from your local utility or a lightning strike nearby, the surge protector will keep your equipment from being ''fried.'' You'll need one surge protector for your electric line and another for your phone line. One without the other leaves your equipment exposed.

You'll also need to have coverage for any inventory you keep on hand. Hopefully, it will be minimal. Again, if you're working out of your home, your homeowner's policy may provide coverage. If not, consult with your insurance agent.

CHOOSING YOUR BUSINESS STRUCTURE

As we learned in chapter 4, one of your biggest decisions will be deciding what business structure to use. Most businesses use one of three options—a sole proprietorship, a partnership, or a corporation. Each structure has different liability and taxation characteristics that will determine which is best for you. You should consult with your attorney and accountant in making your decision.

As we also learned in chapter 4, I strongly feel that *all* businesses, regardless of size or complexity, should incorporate. There's simply too much at stake not to. Nonetheless, roughly 50 percent of small business owners don't follow this advice and operate as sole proprietorships or partnerships. Granted, most of them cruise along comfortably and profitably. But there are also a significant number sitting in tiny apartments, having lost their homes and savings to pay creditors or settle lawsuits and wondering why they never took the few simple steps and spent the relatively modest amount of money that would have kept their worlds from collapsing around them.

Ultimately, you have to decide what business structure is best for you, so here are the basics of all three.

SOLE PROPRIETORSHIP

A sole proprietorship is the simplest and easiest way to start a business. It's also the cheapest. In a proprietorship, you're the boss. You alone are the organizer and operator of the business and the owner of all its assets. Proprietorships require the least accounting and legal work of the three forms. They also pay the lowest taxes.

Advantages of a Sole Proprietorship

One big advantage is its simplicity. In many communities, all you have to do is buy a business license to get started. If you operate the business under a fictitious name, however, you'll have to register the name with the appropriate authority. You'll also need to publish the name in your local paper and state that you're the person behind the business.

Another advantage is you're the only one involved in making decisions. Do you want to offer a new product, change your advertising, or even lay around on the beaches of Mexico for two weeks for a vacation? It's totally up to you. Operating alone also lets you take action quickly. If you see an opportunity, you can jump on it immediately. If you were in a partnership or a corporation, action could be taken only after any number of meetings were held and votes were cast.

Sole proprietorships also have simple forms of organization. You're alone at the top, and everyone reports to you. Neither a partnership nor a corporation will provide you with such autonomy.

Disadvantages of a Sole Proprietorship

The disadvantages of a sole proprietorship are caused by the same thing that makes them attractive—the fact that you're operating alone.

As we learned in chapter 4, the biggest disadvantage—and this is a *big* disadvantage—is liability. You'll be solely responsible for every debt and obligation of the business and have no shelter from creditors or lawsuits. You can protect yourself against many kinds of claims with commercial liability insurance. But as claims against businesses have risen in recent years, so have insurance premiums. If you can't afford them, you shouldn't go into business as a sole proprietor.

Another disadvantage is limited access to capital. Unlike a corporation, you can't offer stock. And you don't have partners to share in business costs. You're limited to the money you can raise on your own. And for most people, that's not a heck of a lot.

Operating alone can also result in incredible stress. You'll be in charge of everything, and the pressure can become overwhelming. Finally, your personal finances and those of your business will always be entwined. The business will never really take on a life of its own.

Tax implications

Owners of sole proprietorships pay taxes as individuals. If they have additional income or loss from other employment or investments, they combine those figures with the profit or loss from their business on one tax form.

PARTNERSHIP

Your second option will be to form a partnership with one or more persons. For instance, if my friend Steve the professor and I were to start our business together, we probably would create a partnership. If anyone else wanted to invest in a share of the business, they, too, would become a partner.

Partnerships can sometimes be a good strategy for people who have a minimal amount of money to invest in a business. If you have a partner like Steve, who's interested in the business more as an investment than as something to be involved with day to day, he or she might be willing to put up the majority of the capital in return for a larger piece of the profits. Your financial contribution would be smaller, but you'd still be the one running the business. The two of you would have to reach an agreement beforehand on an equitable distribution of earnings.

The key ingredients in a partnership are trust and communication, so you'll need to choose your partners with great care. It's a lot like being married. There are many decisions to share and disagreements to work out. Anger and resentment can quickly become overwhelming if the partners are unable to communicate and resolve their differences.

The Uniform Partnership Act

The rights and obligations of each individual in a partnership are spelled out in the Uniform Partnership Act, a model partnership law adopted in its entirety or in part by most states. You should have your attorney check your state's interpretation of the act before you create a partnership.

The act states that each partner has the right to:

- share in the management and conduct of the business;
- share in the profits of the firm;
- receive repayment of contributions;
- receive indemnification for, or return of, payments made on behalf of the partnership;
- receive interest on additional advances made to the business;
- have access to the books and records of the partnership; and
- have formal accounting of partnership affairs.

The act also states that each partner has the obligation to:

- contribute toward losses sustained by the partnership;
- work for the partnership without pay in the traditional sense, but rather for a share of the profits;
- submit to majority vote, or arbitration, when differences arise about the conduct or affairs of the business;
- give other partners any information known personally about partnership affairs; and
- account to the partnership for all profits coming from any partnership transaction, or from the use of partnership property.

Advantages of a partnership

First, you'll have more money. Partners are sources of additional capital. Second, your liability is decreased. The creditors of an individual partner cannot come after property owned by the partnership. They can only attach the interest and income of the individual partners.

An investor in a business can also be what's called a "limited partner." This type of partnership provides special tax advantages and limited liability, and it is usually found in real estate development and international business deals. Being recognized as a limited partner requires some legal hoop jumping and therefore the assistance of a good attorney.

Disadvantages of a partnership

Partners are extremely vulnerable to one another. For example, one partner can commit the partnership to all sorts of legally binding arrangements without the knowledge or consent of the other partners. Let's say Steve the professor suddenly decided we need to lease a $500-a-month Lexus as our company car. He could go out and commit us to the deal, and I might not know anything about it until the payment book showed up. By then, there would be little I could do about it.

Lack of autonomy can also be a disadvantage. Decisions are no longer made based on what's best for you; they're made based on what's best for the organization. They also *should* be made jointly, and this can slow down the speed with which things happen.

Tax implications

The complexity of taxation for partnerships prevents the topic from being completely discussed in this book, but here are a couple of the basics. First, each partner is individually responsible for her share of taxes resulting from the business, and she must file her own income tax return. Second, although partnerships don't file tax returns, they do have to file an information return (Form 1065) signed by one partner. The form reports gross income, deductions, and the percentage of the partnership's profit or loss claimed by each partner. Each partner is then responsible for his or her proportionate amount of taxes.

INCORPORATION

A corporation is the most complex of the three business entities.
It's an artificial being, recognized by law and created by
applying to the secretary of state of whichever state will be
the legal home of the corporation. All fifty states recognize
corporations. But since corporate laws, taxes, and regulations
vary greatly from state to state, a good deal of research is
needed before you decide where to incorporate. Once you apply,
the secretary of state issues you a charter—a license that allows
you to form the corporation and that states you are incorporated.

A corporation is owned by its stockholders. The money they
pay for their stock is used by the corporation for capital. In
return for their investment, they receive a portion of the corporation's profits. These payments are called dividends. In a large,
publicly held corporation, the stock will be owned by thousands
of investors and can be bought or sold through one of the
nation's securities exchanges. In a small, privately held company, however, the stock might be owned by just a few individuals and will not be publicly bought or sold.

A corporation is run by a board of directors chosen by the
stockholders. The day-to-day operation of the business is carried
out by officers—president, vice president, treasurer, and secretary—hired by the board of directors.

Advantages of a corporation

Many people associate incorporation with big business, but in
fact there are no limits on what kind of a business can incorporate. I have a friend who runs a one-person, Jill-of-all-trades
graphic design firm, and she incorporated. So did Jeannie Johnston. Their reason was the same reason why even the owner
of the smallest business should form a corporation—*protection
from liability*.

Remember, a corporation is like an artificial person. If someone sues your business, they sue the corporation, not you, so
your personal property is safe. For example, if you're going to
have to lease commercial real estate for your business, incorporation will protect you from the landlord if the business should

fail or if you have to break the lease for other reasons. If you've signed the lease as an officer of the corporation, the landlord can only go after the assets of the corporation.

Another advantage of incorporation is the ability to raise capital as it's needed by selling additional stock. Although this spreads ownership of the business among more people, you can still control your company by controlling the amount of stock owned by various individuals. As long as you and your associates hold a majority of the stock, you make the decisions.

Incorporation also has a certain cachet for some people. Many businesses, particularly service companies, will incorporate simply to have that "Inc." after their name. If it impresses your customers, so much the better.

Disadvantages of a corporation

Incorporation protects you from creditors. But if you're sued, many creditors will attempt to prove you've operated your business as a sole proprietorship or a partnership rather than as a corporation. This is sometimes called "piercing the corporate shield." For this reason, it's critical that you follow your state's corporate laws and regulations to the letter and keep your personal affairs and corporate affairs separate.

Sophisticated lenders and suppliers will often pierce the corporate shield by requiring you or other stockholders to personally guarantee payment for loans or supplies. They may even send two sets of bills, one to the corporation and one to you.

Another disadvantage is tax liability, as we'll see below.

Tax implications

Like partnership taxation, corporate taxation is too complex to be covered here in detail, but here's the basic problem. Corporations are treated like individuals for federal income tax purposes, and their tax rates are much higher than those for sole proprietorships or partnerships. Corporate profits can also be taxed twice. The corporation pays a tax on its profits before it distributes them to its shareholders, which reduces the amount being distributed. Then the shareholders have to pay a second tax on the profits as personal income. If the shareholders also receive a salary from the corporation, they have to pay a tax on that as well.

One way to avoid double taxation is to form what's called an S Corporation (previously called a Subchapter S Corporation). This allows the corporation, at the request of the shareholders, to set aside the corporate entity and pass profits and losses directly through to the shareholders. A corporation must meet the following requirements to qualify for S status:

- It must be incorporated in the United States.
- No shareholder can be an alien nonresident individual.
- Shareholders must be natural persons, estates, or trusts.
- No shareholder can be a partnership or corporation.
- The corporation can have only one class of common stock, and no preferred stock.
- There must be no more than thirty-five shareholders.

S Corporation status can be particularly advantageous in some cases and a drawback in others. It's a complicated area and requires the services of an experienced tax attorney.

FINDING PROFESSIONAL ASSISTANCE

Behind every successful business venture, there's a key decision-making group engaged in the management of the business. You and any partners will obviously be the key decision makers from day-to-day. But equally important will be your attorney, your accountant, and your banker.

Don't underestimate—or underutilize—their knowledge. A lot of entrepreneurs are mavericks by nature and find it hard to turn to others for help. They think that because they've decided to go into business for themselves, they're now business experts. It doesn't work that way. And the sooner they realize it, the better off they are. *The only way to become an expert is to hire experts.*

WHERE ARE THEY?

The best way to find experts is to ask people who are in the same business you're about to enter. You can also check professional associations. Don't hire people who advertise. If they have enough free time to look for new clients, they're not very good at what they do.

For each position you need to fill, make a list with at least three candidates. Call each one, tell them what you're doing, and ask for a free consultation. If they object, cross them off your list. There are plenty of other people out there who would be happy to have your business.

When you meet with a candidate, look at his office. Is it neat and organized? That usually means he's organized. Does he take phone calls while he's talking to you? If so, it probably means he'll never give your business his full attention.

Ask him about his professional affiliations and ongoing education. All professional fields are constantly changing, and any pro who's worth his hourly fee makes every effort to keep up. Ask him about his other clients. Does he represent anyone else in your field? Listen carefully to his answers. Do they sound packaged, or is he responding honestly and thoughtfully? If you don't feel the two of you can communicate well, thank him for his time and leave.

Ask about his fees. How much does he charge and why? Tell him exactly what you need him to do and ask how many hours he thinks it'll take. When does he bill? His fees are going to be part of your costs, and you'll need to factor them into your business plan.

Before you leave the professional's office, ask for the names of three recent clients whose circumstances are similar to yours. Contact them and ask them about his services. Has his work been satisfactory? Is he efficient and responsive to their needs? Have they gotten along well? Would they hire him again?

Once you've decided on a professional, write an engagement/disengagement letter that spells out what you want the professional to do for you and what you understand his fees to be. Be sure to include a mechanism to separate yourself from the professional if you should decide your affiliation needs to end.

You also need to find someone with whom you have a good rapport. Communication, humor, and shared interests all help smooth any professional relationship. Sophistication and wisdom are pretty valuable, too. You should be able to learn from him and feel comfortable asking about things you don't understand. The two of you need to work as a team. That means he needs to listen to your concerns and look out for your interests. If you get the feeling that to him you're just another fee, go find someone else.

FINDING AN ATTORNEY

A good attorney is expensive but worth every penny. Getting even a small business up and running means navigating through a certain amount of bureaucratic nonsense. An attorney will make this task much easier.

Experience is the key, so the ideal attorney has been around the block a few times. If he's ever run his own business, that's even better. He has to be completely familiar with your situation and sensitive to your needs and wants. An experienced attorney also has many years' worth of contacts he can consult if you run into problems he can't handle. By association, they also become part of your management team.

As a start-up mail-order business endeavor, your legal needs will be minimal. You'll need a certain amount of tax advice and recommendations on business structure. Your attorney will also be familiar with the documents you'll need to fill out and file to start your business. If you're operating from your home, you should have him check the zoning laws and any other restrictions that may impede your business.

FINDING AN ACCOUNTANT

Your accountant will be the other indispensable member of your management team. He can help you prepare budgets and cash flow statements, do business projections, evaluate balance sheets, complete tax forms, and prepare profit and loss statements. He'll also help you determine start-up costs, choose a business structure, create an inventory control procedure, and rate your accounts receivable. And he'll give soothing answers to frantic questions like, Am I making any money yet?

When you look at candidates, choose only Certified Public Accountants (CPAs). These people have earned their titles by undergoing extensive training and passing rigorous exams, so they're universally respected in the business world. In fact, their training has as much to do with ethics as it does with accounting. They're licensed, and, because they can lose their licenses, they are invariably straight arrows. You may even have potential investors demand that you use a CPA before they'll consider your business.

The person you select should be experienced, but that doesn't mean he has to be tottering around with a cane. Many bright young CPAs will work for a large firm for four or five years and then go out on their own. You want someone who's energetic, responsible, precise, and a perfectionist. And, like your attorney, he should be able to teach you a few things.

As a small start-up, your accounting needs, just like your legal needs, will be minimal. You'll probably want some initial advice on setting up a bookkeeping system, and I definitely recommend having an accountant do your taxes. Other than that, you'll probably be able to handle everything yourself. But knowing that advice is just a phone call away will provide you with a great deal of security.

FINDING A BANKER

Banks today are more competitive than ever. Since they're virtually identical in their rules and interest rates, they've made service a priority to attract customers. They'll go out of their way to take care of all your banking needs—from payroll and business checking accounts to IRAs, CDs, and Keoghs. And they'll appoint one banker to take care of you.

Your banker will be the final member of your management team, so you need to search diligently for someone you like and trust. He needs to be learned, experienced, concerned about your needs, and willing to deal with your problems personally. His services will be invaluable. He can provide you with financial advice, help you optimize your cash management, prepare letters of credit, put you in touch with other financial contacts, and generally keep an eye out for your interests.

Both your attorney and your accountant can be good sources of information about various bankers in your area. You can also check the ads to see what banks seem to be interested in your kind of business. You don't have to stay in the area, either. Having to travel out of town on occasion is a small price to pay for good banking service.

WHAT'S NEXT?

Remember the 12 Rules For Doing It Cheaply we discussed in chapter 4? Rule number one is to create a business plan. This will be the road map that will guide your operation day to day. It will also be the document you'll be presenting to lenders and potential partners to convince them that your business is worthy of their investment. We'll look at how to create a business plan in chapter 9.

FOR MORE INFORMATION

Here are several books that will provide you with additional information on business structure, taxation, setting up a home office, and keeping costs down.

* *How to Start a Home Business* by Michael Antoniak (Avon, 1995).
* *Starting On a Shoestring* (3rd edition) by Arnold S. Goldstein (John Wiley & Sons, 1995).
* *Starting and Managing the Small Business* by Arthur H. Kuriloff, John M. Hemphill, Jr., and Douglas Cloud (McGraw-Hill, 1993).
* *Legal Handbook for Small Business* by Marc J. Lane (AMACOM, 1989).
* *Legal Master Guide for Small Business* by Fred S. Steingold (Prentice-Hall, 1983).
* *The Small Business Legal Problem Solver* by Arnold S. Goldstein (Zebra Books, 1986).
* *Incorporating a Small Business* by Allen J. Parker (Practicing Law Institute, New York, 1987).

CREATING A BUSINESS PLAN

I'm a list maker. When I get to my office in the morning, the first thing I do is grab a legal pad and write down all the things I need to do that day. The list includes stories I need to work on, phone calls I need to make, E-mail I need to send, and any other tasks that need to be accomplished. Then during the course of the day, I cross each one off as it's completed. And I try not to leave the office until they're all done.

I do this because it keeps me focused and makes me more productive. These are the same reasons why you need to create a business plan for your mail-order business. A business plan is a master list of goals and tasks that will guide you in your day-to-day running of the business. It will describe your business in detail, including its management, products, marketing, and earnings projections. The more thorough it is, the easier your job will be.

Preparing a business plan serves several other valuable functions. First, it makes you think through *every* aspect of the business and get each one down in writing. If you prepare the plan correctly, nothing will go uninspected.

Second, it will help you distance yourself from the excitement and emotion you feel. Although these feelings are certainly important in helping you get started in business, they could also lead you to ignore things you don't want to recognize. The plan will make you look at the business and your target market from a slightly more sober perspective. You may even discover it isn't such a great idea after all.

And third, the business plan will help you learn whether *you* are up to the task. As you gain a better understanding of just what you're getting yourself into, you may decide you're biting off a bit more than you can chew.

Once you're *in* business, your plan will allow you to step back periodically and take an objective look at how things are progressing. You'll know quickly whether you're on the intended track or whether you've deviated from the original plan. If you find you've somehow gotten pointed in the wrong direction, you can take the proper steps to get back on course.

A business plan has yet another purpose. It's absolutely essential if you're seeking financing or trying to entice partners to join your venture. Lenders want to know as much as possible about the businesses they're being asked to finance, and they'll review your plan very, very carefully. For this reason, a business plan can be a time-consuming document to prepare. Depending on the size and complexity of your business, and whether or not you're seeking outside financing, it could be anywhere from 5 to 100 pages in length.

Make sure you take the time to put your plan together correctly. It can take weeks or even months, depending on the amount of free time you have. If you're still working full-time for someone else, and are only able to work on your plan on weekends, you'll probably need several months to complete it. DON'T RUSH! Keep at it until it's done right.

One other thing. Despite its importance, a business plan is not carved in stone. Every business owner's goals and ideas change over time, reacting either to changes in the marketplace or in the business itself. Your business plan should be adjusted and fine-tuned as often as necessary to reflect these changes.

HOW TO STRUCTURE YOUR BUSINESS PLAN

As befits a small start-up mail-order concern, your business plan will be fairly simple. Nonetheless, like all business plans, it should cover the following basic areas. Because you're starting small, most of the sections will be fairly easy to prepare. Two of them, however, will be particularly critical—financing and marketing.

Cover Page

This section gives an overview of your company—its name, address, and phone number, the names of its owners and officers, and whether it's a sole proprietorship, partnership, or corporation. You also should include the name of the person who prepared the business plan, and you should personalize the plan by including the name of the person or persons receiving it ("This document has been prepared for Mr. Joseph Smith," for example). It can't hurt to stroke their egos a bit.

Make sure your business plan looks professional. It should be printed on quality paper, not handwritten, and bound in an attractive cover. The cover should include the name, address, and phone number of the business. If you have a logo, use it— it adds to the plan's professional appearance and impact.

Description of the Business

Here you'll describe the nature of the business. You'll identify the specific industry the business is in and the products or services it offers.

Describe in a technically accurate manner how your product works or how your service is used. Describe the results of your market tests to show the marketability of your product or service. Describe any future tests you plan on conducting. Also, describe your ideas for future products or services.

Management Structure

This section lists the officers and managers of the business, describes the responsibilities of each, and explains the way the business is structured. You should include an organizational chart showing exactly where the officers and managers fit in the company. You should also include their résumés.

Financial Information

Most start-up mail-order concerns won't be looking for financing, at least not from banks. But if you are, the preparation of this section should receive particularly careful attention. You'll list the amount of money you have to invest in the business, the amount of money you're asking for, and what the money will be used for.

You'll need to convince lenders that your business will generate enough income to pay back the loan, so you'll also need to include a projected profit-and-loss statement, a break-even analysis, and a projected cash flow analysis.

MARKET ANALYSIS

If you've done your market research correctly, this section will paint an accurate picture of exactly who and where your customers are. It will include a demographic description of your customers, describe the market size and trends that indicate your business will succeed, estimate your market share and projected sales, and predict future opportunities for growth. You'll also need to include a detailed analysis of your competition and how they will affect your business.

As we noted earlier in the book, the sales patterns of your product or service may be seasonally influenced. If this is the case, that information should be included in this section as well.

MARKETING STRATEGY

Here you'll include your overall plan for marketing your product. First describe the strategies you'll use to reach your customers, whether direct mail, advertising, or some other method. You might include a sample of an ad, brochure, or other piece of promotional literature. Present data that support your ability to reach your sales goals, including the results of your market tests.

You'll also need to include your pricing structure. Again using the results of your market tests, you can show how your prices were determined and that your projected sales can be achieved at those price levels.

Customer service will be an important part of your business, so you'll need to describe your policies for returns, credits, refunds, etc.

PLAN OF OPERATION

In this section you'll describe exactly how the business will be operated. This will include the location of your business, a list of equipment and a description of its function, your inventory control and distribution methods, the number and functions of your employees, and the wages you plan on paying them.

TIMETABLES AND SCHEDULES

Efficient timing is critical to getting any business off the ground. The sooner you're in business, the sooner you'll make money. This section will include a detailed schedule of all the tasks needed to get the business up and running and when those tasks will be completed.

Include a three-year plan for the growth of the business. If you're expecting to gross $25,000 in sales the first year, you might want to make your target for the second year $30,000; for the third year, $35,000. Also, make sure your schedule includes any deadlines or major events that will affect the business.

SUPPORTING DATA

In this section you'll include any materials that will further explain the goals or operation of your business. These materials can include articles about trends in the mail-order industry or in your target market, additional product literature, charts and graphs, and any other information that will further explain your business and its goals.

CALCULATING START-UP COSTS

One thing your business plan should tell you is the total amount of money you'll need to start the business. This chart will help you calculate your costs. It's based on you starting the business at home.

EXPENSE	COST

Business license _____
Other fees _____
Insurance
  Home _____
  Equipment _____
  Auto _____
  Other _____
Professional consultation
  Attorney fees _____
  Accountant fees _____
  Other _____
Office expenses
  Desk and chair _____
  Telephone line(s) _____
  Other utility connections _____
  Lighting _____
  Cabinets _____
  Shelving _____
  Renovation _____
  Misc. (pens, paper, etc.) _____
Equipment
  Telephone _____
  Fax machine _____
  Answering machine _____
  Computer _____
  Software _____
  Printer _____
Advertising/Promotion
  Stationery _____
  Business cards _____
  Logo _____
  Newspaper advertising _____
  Magazine advertising _____
  Direct mail advertising _____
Inventory _____
Shipping materials
  Boxes _____

Paper	_____
Tape	_____
Other	_____

TOTAL COSTS   **_____**

CALCULATING CASH FLOW

Another important task in creating your business plan is running a cash flow analysis. It'll help you see if this pipe dream of yours can actually generate the money you want it to.

And if you think your analysis is important to you, wait until you see how important it is to your potential lenders. Sure, they want to see that your business is capable of earning what you need. But what they're really interested in is seeing that there's enough left over to pay *them* back.

One thing you need to realize is that just because a business is doing well doesn't mean it has a lot of cash on hand. For example, a business that extends credit to its customers can enjoy wonderful sales, but until its customers actually pay their bills, all it has to show for its success is a lot of accounts receivable. And accounts receivable won't pay for groceries. This is why one of the 12 Rules For Doing It Cheaply is "cash only." When someone buys something from you, you'll want their money in your hot little hand as quickly as possible.

Your cash flow analysis should chart your income and expenditures, month by month, for your first year of business. These figures will come from your projections of sales and expenses, and they must be carefully timed to make sure you can meet your financial obligations on schedule.

When it comes right down to it, it's really not that different from budgeting your home expenses. You know how often you get paid (weekly, biweekly, monthly), so you organize paying your bills and shopping around that schedule. Of course, if you're terrible at budgeting your personal finances, you may find this news rather disconcerting. Just remember what I pointed out in chapter 3: If you're uncomfortable dealing with money, this is the perfect time to face your fears and begin doing it right.

You should enlist your accountant's assistance in preparing your cash flow analysis. Whatever form he chooses to use is fine, provided he follows these basic steps. Remember, you'll be preparing a report for each month.

Step 1—Calculate Total Cash Available

A. **Calculate your cash on hand.** Enter the amount you expect to have in your accounts at the beginning of the month, whether from earnings, loans, or other sources.
B. **Calculate your cash receipts.** These will include:
   • **cash sales**—Enter the amount you estimate you'll be paid in cash, check, or money order.
   • **credit card sales**—Enter the amount you expect to earn from credit card orders, less the bank or card company fee.
   • **other cash receipts**—This could be from short-term loans or other sources.
C. Add A and B to calculate your **total cash available**.

Step 2—Calculate Cash Expenditures. This includes monthly expenses as well as capital purchases.

A. **Loan payments.** Include all monthly loan payments, including interest and principal.
B. **Capital purchases.** Include items like electronic equipment or packaging equipment you purchase for the business.
C. **Inventory.** Include the amount you'll spend to purchase your product or products.
D. **Operating expenses.** Include utility bills, professional services, insurance premiums, and other expenses incurred by the business.
E. **Withdrawals.** This includes salary you pay yourself or others, income tax payments, social security payments, health insurance premiums, etc.
F. Add A, B, C, D, and E to calculate your **total cash expenditures**.

If your cash available is greater than your cash expenditures, you have a positive cash flow. If your expenditures are greater than your available cash, however, you have a negative cash flow. Should you expect a positive cash flow every month? Not necessarily, although it would be nice. There certainly may be months in which a large expense such as the purchase of a piece of equipment might keep you in the red. However, those months should be the exception, not the rule.

But if you find that in the normal course of business, your projections show month after month of negative cash flow, you're in trouble. Since you're operating with cash payments only, this means your business will be a losing proposition. This is a perfect example of how doing a business plan can help you see problems before they actually occur. If your cash flow analysis indicates an ongoing negative cash flow, you can try to restructure the two sides of the equation to the point where you at least break even. If you can't do that, you'll know it's time to find some other business to go into.

FINDING HELP

Preparing a business plan can seem like a daunting task, particularly if you've never done it before. But there are a number of sources that offer assistance. Several computer software programs are available that are designed to create business plans. The Small Business Association can give you a list of experienced business plan consultants. Another good source of help is the Service Corps of Retired Executives (SCORE), which provides professional assistance under the auspices of the SBA. For particular areas within your business plan, you should consult your attorney, your accountant, and your banker.

WHAT'S NEXT?

You've selected a product or service, tested the market, created a business plan, and set up your business. Now there's nothing

left to do but start selling. That means getting your customers'
attention and convincing them you're offering the hottest thing
on the market. We'll take a look at how to reach them in
chapter 10.

FOR MORE INFORMATION

Here are several books that can help you with your business
plan.

- *How to Prepare and Present a Business Plan* by Joseph Man-
  cuso (Simon & Schuster, 1992).
- *Building Your Business Plan: A Step-by-Step Approach* by
  Harold J. McLaughlin (John Wiley & Sons, 1985).
- *How to Develop a Business Plan in 15 Days* by William M.
  Luther (American Management Association, 1987).
- *The Business Planning Guide: Creating a Plan for Success in
  Your Own Business* by David H. Bangs (Upstart Publishing
  Co., 1992).
- *Total Business Planning: A Step-by-Step Guide With Forms*
  by E. James Burton (John Wiley & Sons, 1988).

GETTING YOUR CUSTOMERS' ATTENTION

Welcome to the world of advertising! It's a fascinating place, where psychology, sociology, demographics, art, technology, and a little bit of magic are combined to entice people into paying money for all sorts of things. The question of whether or not they *need* the items they buy is immaterial. What *is* important is the fact that they *want* the items they buy. It's the job of advertising to develop that desire.

I find advertising one of the most fascinating parts of our culture. For example, if you watch the Super Bowl every year, you'll notice that there's much more than just football going on. The evening has also become the Super Bowl of advertising. Some of the biggest brand names in the country—Pepsi, Coke, Nike, Reebok, Budweiser—vie for the nation's attention with the debut of new ads. These ads are the result of months and months of creative fervor and millions of dollars and are designed to set consumers on their ears. They don't always work, but when they do, they're marvels to watch and listen to. In fact, they're usually a lot more interesting than the game itself. People still talk about Apple Computer's "1984" ad that unveiled the Macintosh computer, even though it aired only once.

The media pay close attention, too, devoting a great deal of time before the game to speculating on who's doing what. And in the days following the game, newspapers and magazines—as well as conversations around the water cooler—are filled with analyses and opinions on which companies had the best ads.

Unfortunately, the ads for your little mail-order business

won't attract quite as much attention. But that doesn't mean you can't be every bit as creative or have as much fun as the big boys. If you have any sort of a flair for writing or graphic design, you'll have a great time with this aspect of your business.

DOING IT YOURSELF

Obviously, the cheapest way to approach your advertising is to do it yourself. Hiring copywriters and graphic artists is expensive, so writing your own ad copy and doing your own layout are critical to keeping costs down. But before you put pen to paper, there's one step that's equally important.

Ⓢ SET UP YOUR OWN ADVERTISING AGENCY

If you're going to create your own advertising, your first step should be to set up your own agency, and for a very good reason. Most publications give agencies a commission, usually 15 percent, for bringing them business. So when you approach a publication as an agency, you're getting a 15 percent discount on your ad rate.

Setting up an agency is simple enough. Just think up a name, have some letterhead printed, and deal with advertisers as a representative of the agency, not your mail-order business. The savings will quickly add up.

You may occasionally run into a publication that says it won't accept ads from in-house advertising agencies. But few actually go to the trouble to follow up on their rule. It's simply too much trouble to check. Besides, most of them have the rule just to keep the big ad houses happy. However, it might be a good idea to use a separate address and a separate checking account for your agency business.

Another advantage to setting up an agency is the opportunity to do work for other people. If you have copywriting talents, for example, you may find a lot of people eager to have you create ad copy for them. It's usually not terribly time-consuming, and it can be a nice addition to your income. If it goes really well, you may find you suddenly have a whole new business on your hands.

Understanding Your Customers

Today's buyers are, for the most part, critical and demanding consumers. They live in a media-saturated culture, and are constantly deluged with advertising from television, radio, magazines and newspapers, billboards and signs, the mail, and even the telephone. (Take the time to count the number of advertising messages you encounter in a single day. You'll be amazed.) They've seen and heard it all, and as a result, they've developed a tough skin resistant to a lot of what's thrown at them. Your job is to get through that shell and get them to notice your product.

Once you do, you need to entice them into buying. If you're selling an item that's only $5 or $10, you'll probably have an easier time than with a $100 item. This is particularly true in times of economic downturn. When jobs and money are tight, people by necessity cut down on their spending.

Good advertising speaks to potential buyers in language they understand. If your product is targeted to well-educated, affluent customers, you must reflect that in your advertising. Use words and images they're familiar with. But if your market is more of a cross section of the socioeconomic spectrum, that, too, must be accounted for in your advertising strategy.

The bottom line to all this is you need to know who your customers are, understand the factors that influence their buying habits, and incorporate that information into your advertising and marketing.

Motivating Your Customers

One of the downsides of selling by mail is the fact that your customer can't examine the product in person. Another is the fact that you can't meet a customer face-to-face to explain the product and answer questions. That means you sink or swim with your advertising.

The trick, then, is to motivate your customers to act with just the wording in your ad. Some ads will literally do just that by urging consumers to Act Now! or Order Today! or Buy While Supplies Last! This tactic, though hardly subtle, does work with some customers by making them think they're going to lose out if they don't move quickly.

Another common strategy is to offer something free with each purchase. Some people can't pass up a freebie, and the chance to get a free pen, calendar, or money clip will frequently be enough to entice them to fill out an order form and send in a check. If you do offer a free item, though, make sure it's something with universal appeal or usefulness. Otherwise, you're attracting only part of your customer base.

You also can offer a free bonus gift without saying what the gift is. Oddly enough, there's a certain type of consumer who will respond to that sort of an offer just to find out what the mystery gift might be. Their curiosity gets the best of them. (It's also a good way to get rid of inventory that hasn't sold well. I know of a guy who unloaded 2,000 New York Jets key rings with this very strategy.)

Of course, the most common approach is to make customers think they're saving money by ordering in response to a particular ad. "One-Time Offer!" and "Prices Slashed!" and "Order Now Before Prices Increase!" are just a few of the grabbers that mail-order firms use to attract thrifty buyers.

WHAT ADVERTISING METHODS SHOULD YOU USE?

If you're a fan of the television comedy *News Radio,* you're familiar with station owner Jimmy James and his concern about getting the most bang for his buck. You're going to have the same concern. Advertising is expensive, and if you're paying money for advertising that's not bringing you business, you're not getting much bang for *your* buck. You might as well throw your money out the window. Let's take a look at various forms of advertising and see which are right for a small start-up mail-order business.

⑨ Classified Ads

Almost all small mail-order operators use classified ads when they first go into business. They're very inexpensive, and, as we learned from the test marketing in chapter 7, they're usually quite efficient, generating the most responses for the least money.

Classifieds are short ads printed in very small type, usually three to ten lines long and a column wide, with no artwork or illustrations, and they are found in the backs of virtually all newspapers and many magazines. How cheap are they? Well, the paper in my town sometimes charges as little as $6.50 for a three-line ad for six days. And every day that paper is probably seen by at least 40,000 people. That's pretty good exposure for just pennies.

Classified ads are perfect for mail order for a variety of reasons. As we've already seen, they're inexpensive. Also, they're easy to plan and write, they're a good way to test products, and they reach tons of people. And best of all, you can create them yourself.

The best classified ads begin with a short sentence printed in bold type to get the reader's attention. Here's an example of an attention-grabber for a mail-order business selling ice hockey equipment:

THE PUCK STOPS HERE! But your buck goes a lot further! We guarantee the lowest prices on hockey equipment in the Northeast. All major manufacturers. Send $1.00 for catalog to (company name and address).

I have a fourteen-year-old son who lives and breathes hockey, and believe me, his eye would zero in on this ad like radar on an incoming 757. Within a few days, the catalog would be sitting on our coffee table. (And within a few weeks, the company would probably have some of my money.)

When you use classifieds to advertise your product, you need to decide whether you're using the ad to actually sell your product or, like the hockey equipment ad, to get the reader to contact you for more information. (That's called the inquiry and follow-up method. It's discussed later in this chapter.)

If you're planning on selling directly from classified ads, you should have a product or products that sell for $10 or less. This is because there's generally a direct correlation between the price of a product and the amount of space needed to advertise it. This makes sense if you think about it for a moment. For example, which of these two classified ads doesn't seem quite right?

NATIONAL FOOTBALL LEAGUE TRADING CARDS. 1990-95 rosters. $5 per package of 6. Send check or money order to (company name and address).

MUSEUM QUALITY DIAMOND AND RUBY NECKLACES! World's finest stones. $6,500 each! 2 for $12,500! 3 for $18,000! Act now! Send check or money order to (company name and address).

The first one seems okay, but the second one? I don't know about you, but I can't ever recall seeing a classified ad from a mail-order company selling expensive jewelry. This is the type of product you'll see sold in a full-page ad in the *New York Times* or *Vanity Fair* or *Town and Country*. The ad will include an enticing photograph of the necklace—probably draped around the neck of a beautiful model— and sexy ad copy to make it seem absolutely irresistible. These are very expensive items targeted at well-to-do people. They're given the space and graphic look needed to get the attention of buyers.

So the classifieds are really the blue-collar neighborhood of the advertising world. But that doesn't mean everything sold in them has to be inexpensive. If you have a flair for copywriting and you're willing to spend a little money on a slightly larger ad, you might just be able to move some merchandise. You'll never know if you don't try. And there's no cheaper place to try than the classifieds.

DISPLAY ADS

These are ads that run throughout the inside of a magazine or newspaper. They can be as small as one inch high by a column wide or as large as a two-page spread. They are priced accordingly.

Display ads give you more room for creativity than a classified ad. You can use artwork or photography, include more copy, and play around with different type styles and sizes. Display ads are more expensive, but as we just learned, you sometimes need to spend a bit more on advertising if you're selling a more expensive product.

INQUIRY AND FOLLOW-UP

The inquiry-and-follow-up method is a commonly used strategy to get your customers' attention for very little money. You run a short ad—usually just a few lines—informing people about your product, and you include an address or phone number they can contact to get more details. If a customer is interested and contacts you, then you send back a letter accompanied by your more expensive promotional literature and an order form.

Here are a few examples of inquiry-and-follow-up ads.

QUIT SMOKING IN 7 DAYS! Our foolproof method has helped thousands! Free brochure! Write to (company name and address) or call (phone number).

MAKE MONEY AT HOME! Add to your income in your spare time. No investment required. Send $1.00 for information packet. (Company name and address).

HEY, BIGFOOT! Having trouble finding shoes that fit? We carry a complete line of hard-to-find sizes. Dress, casual, and athletic shoes. Famous brands. Catalog $2.00. Write or call (company name, address, and phone number).

Inquiry-and-follow-up ads can be classified or display ads. Many companies that use this strategy, like those in the second and third examples, will charge a small amount for their catalog or materials. This may not be the best customer relations, but it's unavoidable when you have thousands of follow-up responses. The costs of producing the materials and mailing them out adds up. Charging for them helps companies recoup some of those costs.

When you get a response to an ad and send the customer your material, there's no guarantee it will produce an order. The inquiry has done what it was designed to do—pique the customer's interest. But it's up to your catalog or other literature to finish the sale. This means that special care must be given in preparing these materials. They must be attractive and creatively written. And the more expensive the product, the fancier the sales literature should be. You also can augment the literature with a little personal contact. For example, a follow-up phone call can sometimes speed things along, particularly if you're selling an unusually expensive item.

The major disadvantage to the inquiry-and-follow-up method is the time it frequently takes to generate an order. Weeks, if not months, can go by from the time of your initial mailing until an order is finally received.

It's important to remember, though, that if someone requests your literature but doesn't get back to you, it doesn't necessarily mean that he is no longer a prospective customer. Sometimes it takes a second or third letter or a phone call or two to inspire him to place an order. If he still doesn't buy, you at least have his name and address on file for subsequent product offerings.

TELEVISION

Some of my favorite mail-order ads are the ones you see on television late at night. You can find them on almost any channel, but the best ones are usually found in the nether regions of the cable lineup. They're the ones with the fast-talking announcers speaking with an urgency that suggests you'd BETTER ACT NOW BECAUSE YOUR LIFE WILL NEVER BE

THE SAME ONCE YOU HAVE THIS WONDERFUL PROD-
UCT IN YOUR HOME!

They sell all sorts of things, but my favorites are the oddball
kitchen gadgets—the knives that cut through cans and the electric gizmos that do all sorts of obscene things to vegetables.
They're all priced at $19.95 and can be purchased by CALLING
THE 800 NUMBER YOU SEE ON YOUR SCREEN NOW!

Television ads are very effective marketing tools for all sorts
of mail-order products. They're so effective, in fact, that they
inspired a whole new approach to selling. Two companies, the
Home Shopping Network and the QVC (Quality, Value, and
Convenience) Network, now offer a twenty-four-hour-a-day display of clothing, jewelry, electronic equipment, kitchen gadgets,
and many other items. Like buying from a catalog, all you
need is your telephone and your trusty credit card to make
a purchase.

Of course, the downside to television advertising is the expense. It's not a medium you're going to be using as a small
start-up business. But down the road, if things go well, it definitely merits looking into. Just make sure you carefully analyze
your demographic target, and make sure your expensive ad is
going to generate enough business to justify its cost. Also, the
price of ads is tied to the size of the local market and the time
of day the ads run. If you're in a small to medium-sized town,
you may find that advertising rates are fairly reasonable in non-
prime-time hours. You also can frequently buy advertising
through your local cable operator and arrange for it to be shown
on specific stations in the cable lineup. In my town, for example, I've noticed a lot of ads for local businesses on ESPN
and CNN.

RADIO

Because it's comparatively inexpensive, radio is a popular medium for many mail-order businesses. The ones that enjoy the
best responses are the ones that tie in their products with specific radio programs. A show on health and nutrition, for example, is a good advertising venue for mail-order businesses that

sell vitamins and nutritional supplements. A program that features oldies would be a good spot for mail-order businesses selling compact discs of hits from the fifties and sixties.

One good strategy for mail-order operators is to work what's called a "per inquiry" deal with a radio station. This involves identifying airtime that the station is using for fluff because it has neither the advertising nor the programming to fill it. A carefully worded letter to the station management explaining how they can increase their profits by running ads for your business will often get their attention. The catch? Rather than a flat ad rate, you pay them an agreed-upon amount for each inquiry the ad generates. It can be an excellent deal for you both.

Many advertisers, and not just mail-order operators, like radio advertising because it generates quick responses. This, in turn, means your money isn't tied up for too long. The downside is that it requires careful monitoring. An ad that's not doing its job must be identified and pulled quickly to avoid unnecessary costs.

FAX MACHINES

It should come as no surprise that the proliferation of fax machines in the United States has been accompanied by a proliferation of merchandisers delivering advertisements via fax. For many companies, fax advertising has proven so successful that it's become a significant marketing tool.

To work well, a faxed ad must be to the point (never more than one page) and not cluttered up with a lot of copy. The copy that does exist should be large enough to be legible on the faxed copy. The ad should reproduce well in black and white (most color ads won't, by the way) and leave room for the sender's identification to print clearly on the receiver's end.

To keep your costs down, you should send faxes during non-business hours. (This is one reason a fax machine with a programmable timer is a good idea. You can set the machine up and go home for the evening.) And it doesn't matter whether anyone is at the other end to receive them. If everyone's out of the office, your advertisement will be there when they return.

One word of caution: Many businesspeople claim to have had good responses from faxed advertisements. But I also know a lot of *recipients* of faxed ads who are driven nuts by the practice. To many people, faxed ads are almost as annoying as the direct marketing phone calls that arrive just when you're sitting down to dinner. I suspect the faxes that work best are the ones that are the most accurately targeted. Therefore, my suggestion is to use faxed ads very selectively and only send them to people you know will be likely purchasers of your product. The fact that they cost money is another good reason to use them selectively.

⑤ THE INTERNET

Since you already have a computer, setting up a web site for your business is easy. You just need a modem, which you may have already purchased (if not, you can buy one for less than $200); a phone line dedicated solely to your computer, since you'll want your web site open twenty-four hours a day; and an Internet connection and E-mail address, which will run about $20 a month. You can learn how to create your own web page (I've done one—it's much easier than you'd think) or hire someone to do it for you. There are many people, including a lot of young and talented graphic designers, offering this service for a fairly inexpensive price. If you don't want to learn how to do it yourself, you should be able to get a single, basic page designed for $250 or less.

Once your page is up and running, you'll have an electronic advertisement that's accessible by every computer user who's connected to the Internet. If someone wants to buy from you, they simply E-mail you an order form with a credit card number. It's a remarkably simple process that, as I said earlier in the book, is about to revolutionize the way we buy and sell goods and services. We'll discuss doing business on the Internet in detail in the next chapter.

REMEMBER TO KEY YOUR ADS

We talked about the importance of keying your ads when we talked about testing in chapter 7. As you experiment with different ad copy and different advertising venues, you'll discover that some are very productive, some are so-so, and others are a waste of money. You'll find out this information by inserting keys into your address. These are numbers or letters or terms that will let you know which responses come from which ads.

There are any number of ways to key an ad. Some mail-order operators prefer to use "departments." It looks rather impressive to the reader because it makes your business seem larger and more complex than it probably is. Let's say you're selling golf accessories and trying a new ad in the *New York Times,* the *Wall Street Journal,* and *USA Today.* Everything in the three ads would be identical except the keys, which would read "Dept. NYT1," "Dept. WS1," and "Dept. USA1." Later, if you decide to try a second ad in the three papers, your keys would be "Dept. NYT2," "Dept. WS2," and "Dept. USA2." If you try a third, all the ads get a "3." Maybe you'll decide to try a fourth ad in the magazines *Golf Digest* and *Golf for Women.* In that case the keys would be "Dept. GD4" and "Dept. GW4."

Over time, your keying system will allow you to gauge the drawing power of different ads as well as analyze the response from the readership of different publications. In the example above, the second ad may generate better response than the first or the third. You might also discover that, for whatever reason, none of the three drew much response from *New York Times* readers. So you've learned two things: ad number 2 will bring you the most business, and you're probably wasting your money advertising your product in the *Times.*

There are any number of ways to key your ads, so use whatever system makes sense to you. Just make sure it allows you to keep accurate records. You're setting up a system that will gather information that's vital to operating your business efficiently and profitably. If your information gets misinterpreted, you'll be spending your valuable advertising dollars in the wrong places and for the wrong ads.

USING DIRECT MAIL

As any mail carrier will tell you, direct mail is an extremely popular marketing strategy for thousands of mail-order businesses. Each year, billions of catalogs, brochures, flyers, letters, circulars, and oversized and overstuffed envelopes make their way into American homes. They range from crude, single-sheet flyers sent out by small time mom-and-pop mail-order operations to complex, multi-component mailings like the slickly packaged and prepared Publisher's Clearinghouse Sweepstakes. Even the Democratic and Republican National Committees use direct mail to appeal to their constituents.

Direct mail is very similar to the inquiry-and-follow-up strategy. The big difference is that in direct mail you're including all your literature, including an order form, in one package. Direct mail is effective. It's also expensive.

Because of the expense involved, the key to success in direct mail is accurate targeting of your mailing. With the inquiry-and-follow-up method, you're sending out an inexpensive mailing almost at random knowing that the people who are truly interested in your product will contact you for more information. In direct mail, however, you need to know who those people are *before* you send out your materials. The key to this is the mailing list.

THE CRITICAL FACTOR: MAILING LISTS

A mailing list is a compilation of *qualified* buyers for your product or service. What's a qualified buyer? It's a person who's a known mail-order shopper with a documented interest in what you're offering and the financial wherewithal to pay for it. When you buy or rent a well-prepared mailing list, every name on it is a qualified buyer who could end up sending you some money.

Where can you get mailing lists?

Mailing lists can be obtained from companies called list brokers. These companies compile lists of people who purchase goods and services by mail order, group the names by product category, and make the lists available to whoever's interested in reaching those groups. Prices usually start at around $50 per 1,000 names. Some companies will require you to purchase a minimum of 5,000 names. The better a list is prepared, the more useful it will be to your business.

For example, if you're selling a new product aimed at golfers, a list broker might sell you a list of names compiled from golf magazine subscription lists, from other businesses (not just mail order) selling golf-related products, and maybe even from the membership lists of golf clubs around the country.

Most of the country's major list brokers are in New York City and Chicago. The best way to determine the quality of their lists is to write for information and prices. Ask them how they obtain their lists and how up-to-date they keep them. If a firm is legitimate, they'll be more than happy to give you whatever information you need. If they're reluctant to discuss their practices with you, find another broker.

Here are the names and addresses of several well-known mailing list brokers:

Dependable Lists
333 N. Michigan Ave.
Chicago, IL 60601

Dunhill Lists, Inc.
419 Park Ave. South
New York, NY 10016

The Kleid Company
200 Park Ave.
New York, NY 10016

MDC List Management
41 Kimler Drive
Hazlewood, MO 63043

Names Unlimited
183 Madison Ave.
New York, NY 10016

National Business Lists
295 Madison Ave.
New York, NY 10017

Other good sources of names and addresses for mailing lists are the membership rosters of organizations and associations (some will sell you a directory), civic and professional groups, college and university student and faculty directories, government lists, magazine subscription lists, and financial rating lists.

Before buying from a list broker, consider the following questions.

- Have you thoroughly investigated the broker's company and its reputation in the industry?

- Has the broker been forthcoming with answers to all your questions?

- How old is the list?
- Has the broker kept names and addresses up to date?
- How does the rental or purchase price compare to what other brokers charge for similar lists?
- Have other mail-order operators had positive results with the broker's lists?
- Do the demographic and socioeconomic characteristics of the people on the list match your product or service?
- When was the last time the broker sold the list to someone selling an item similar to what you're selling?

Should you buy or rent your lists?

For my money, it's easier to rent a list. To ensure maximum response, a mailing list must be constantly monitored to make sure it reflects changes of address, name changes, and people who have passed away (I like to call these folks "terminal customers"). It's a time-consuming job. If you buy a list, you're responsible for doing it. I think it's easier to let the broker worry about keeping it up-to-date.

Can you get burned with mailing lists?

You bet you can! A list is only as good as the firm that prepared it. If you're dealing with a broker who's sloppy in putting his lists together or doesn't stay on top of putting in address and name changes and deleting terminal customers, you're not going to get very good results with your mailing. Even golfers, who are among the most rabid purchasers of mail-order products, finally stop buying when they kick the bucket.

Mailing lists don't come with guarantees. A poor-quality list may cost you hundreds, if not thousands, of dollars in wasted mailings. But if you're unhappy with its performance, you'll have little recourse other than to complain to the broker. You're not going to get your money back, much less any financial consideration for the losses he may have caused you. This is

why it's so important to check out a firm before you purchase
its list.

Mailing by zip code

Mail-order firms whose customers fall within a very defined
socioeconomic group will frequently use zip codes to direct
their mailings. This is because people of similar economic
means tend to cluster together in their own neighborhoods.

Let's say you have a terrific product that, by virtue of its
high price, is affordable only to people with fairly substantial
incomes. If the wealthier neighborhoods in your target market
are clearly defined with their own zip codes, you can direct
your mailing to addresses within those zip codes. By doing this,
you'll reach the types of people who can afford your product.

This tactic, although a good one, really works only in fairly
large cities that are divided up by zip code. In smaller towns
where there may be just a single zip code, it's impossible to
differentiate between neighborhoods.

Creating your own mailing list

Of course, the best list you can ask for is the one you'll create
with the names and addresses of the people who buy from you.
This list will grow steadily over time and, since it's made up
of past customers, should always be your best performer.

As the owner of the list, however, you'll need to work hard
to keep it current. The best way to do this is to always include
a change of address form with your literature. When someone
moves, the post office will only forward mail from their old
address for a few months. After that, if you haven't obtained
their new address, you'll lose them.

Should you sell or rent your lists?

Sure, as long as you're not selling to someone whose product
is in direct competition with yours. Mailing lists are extremely
valuable assets in the mail-order business. You should make as
much money from yours as you can.

What's in a Direct Mail Package?

Most direct mail packages include a cover letter, promotional literature, an order form, and a reply envelope. The contents are then mailed in an outer envelope. Each part of the package has a carefully defined purpose and should be carefully and thoughtfully prepared.

The cover letter

The most important part of the package is the cover letter. It must immediately attract your customers' attention, so it should get right to the point and explain why your product is important to them. This is because your package will almost always be viewed with suspicion when it is received. Your customers won't have the slightest idea what's in it, but they *will* know it means someone's trying to get their money. Your cover letter has to cut through that suspicion quickly. If you get their attention with the first few sentences or paragraphs, the chances are good they'll finish the rest of the letter.

A good cover letter will include your logo on attractively designed letterhead. Use 8½-by-11-inch letter-sized paper. While black ink on white paper is the most inexpensive way to print your letterhead, the addition of a second color will make it seem more professional and will generally draw a better response. You can also experiment with different color stock. (Studies have been done on people's psychological reactions to different colors. Light shades of blue work well with both sexes. Pink and light yellow work well with women. Red, however, is a definite no-no. It's too hard to read, as are the darker shades of most colors.)

Your cover letter should present your product and your arguments for why the customer should buy it—and no more. The reason for this is simple. People don't have a lot of time, and the longer your letter, the more imposing it is to your customer. I'm sure you've opened mailings and pulled out five- and six-page cover letters that seem so intimidating (and time-consuming) that you've thrown them right in the trash.

When you're writing the cover letter, make sure the copy is

crisp and to the point. Keep your sentences and paragraphs short. Try to appeal to people's emotions and desires. Put a space between paragraphs, and underline key words for emphasis.

Promotional literature

If your letter does its job, the customer will then take a look at your promotional literature. This can be anything from a second 8½-by-11-inch flyer to a multipage, four-color brochure. Again, like the cover letter, it should be visually energetic, the copy should be crisp and exciting, and it should immediately make apparent why your product is worth your customers' money.

Promotional literature takes over where the cover letter leaves off. It describes your product in greater detail and demonstrates why it's such a great buy. Illustrations or photographs show the customer exactly what it looks like. Testimonials—statements about the quality of your product from previously satisfied customers—are often useful. The literature will also include the price of your product, in a prominent location and in large type. Don't make customers hunt for a price. It could lead them to believe you're trying to hide it.

The order form

Order forms are more important than you might think. Salespeople who work one-on-one with customers talk about "closing the sale." This is when, after presenting the product and discussing its merits and the customer's needs, the salesperson closes in for the kill, so to speak. He asks the customer to purchase the product.

Your order form can serve the same purpose. Properly prepared, it can continue the work of the cover letter and the promotional literature. It can repeat the strengths of the product and the reasons it will benefit the customer and then ask the customer to fill in their name, address, and method of payment. The copy might read something like this:

YES! I'm ready to spend less time in the kitchen and more time enjoying the things I love to do! Please send me my *Magic Kitchen Helper* **TODAY!**

Please mail to

Name _

Street Address _

City _ _ _ _ _ _ _ _ _ _ _ State _ _ _ _ Zip _ _ _ _ _

I have enclosed a check _ _ _ _ money order _ _ _ as payment.

Please charge my VISA _ _ _ _ _ _ _ _ _ _ _ _ _ _ _ _ _ _

Master Card _ _ _ _ _ _ _ _ Expiration _ _ _ _ _ _ _

Signature _

Order forms can be any size. They can also be self-mailers, or they can be returned in a reply envelope. Some mail-order operators include the order form right on their cover letter or in their promotional material. The form is usually outlined with a dotted line to make sure it stands out from the rest of the page. For the convenience of your customers, you might have their names and addresses preprinted on the form before you mail it to them.

Reply envelope

The reply envelope is more a convenience to your customers than anything else. It keeps them from having to look around for their own envelope after they've filled out the order form. You can use a standard-size letter envelope or the slightly longer business reply envelope.

It's also a nice touch to make the envelope postage paid, although during the start-up period of your business this is really an expense you can do without. And it won't affect your sales. Experience has shown that if a customer wants to make a purchase, they won't be turned off by having to use their own stamp to send in the order form.

CATALOGS

Catalogs are like paper storefronts. You can open the cover and spend hours meandering through the pictures and descriptions of all the merchandise a business has to offer. Catalogs can range from eight- or twelve-page black-and-white cheapies to the expensive, four-color publications put out by mail-order giants like L. L. Bean and J. C. Penney.

Many of the decisions affecting direct mail literature—artwork, color, copy, etc.—also apply to catalogs. Other decisions, such as placement of the merchandise in the publication, are unique to catalogs. Most merchandisers place the best-selling items in the front. And they'll only offer items whose sales potential promises to repay the investment in paper, printing, artwork, and postage.

As customers respond to the merchandise in a catalog, merchandisers will keep track of which items are selling well and which are selling poorly. They'll use this information to move items around in subsequent catalogs, to decide which items to offer at sale prices and which items to discontinue altogether.

The catalog is the cornerstone for thousands of mail-order businesses. For the small start-up business, however, they're a long way in the future. If your business grows and you branch out into multiple offerings, a small catalog may eventually be useful. Just keep in mind they're expensive and require extremely accurate mailing lists. (For more information on catalog marketing for small businesses, see *Home-Based Catalog Marketing* by William J. Bond, McGraw-Hill, Inc., 1993.)

$ DIRECT MAIL POSTAGE

When it comes to postage, I'm a cheapskate. I see no reason to pay for first-class delivery unless it's urgent to get your mailing in the hands of your customers by a certain date. Even then, if you plan your mailing carefully and maintain your production schedule, you should be able to meet any date you set for yourself.

As far as I'm concerned, third class is just fine for direct mailings. It takes longer to get to your customer, but you can factor that into your mailing date. Some people think that customers are sensitive to what kind of postage was used for a mailing. But if that's the case, and I really question whether it is, I think it only occurs when the mailing is for particularly expensive merchandise. Most mail-order operators will tell you they get as good a response, if not better, with third class as they do with first. And they save a lot of money in the process.

Timing Your Direct Mailing

Although there's no agreed-upon perfect day to send out a direct mailing, there is unanimous agreement on when *not* to do it. Never send out a mailing so that it arrives during the first week of the month. Why? Because that's when most bills are sent out. And nothing will kill the spending urge of a consumer faster than opening a stack of bills. If your mailing is the next thing in the pile, it'll go in the trash with hardly a glance.

Ultimately, the type of postage you use will determine your mailing date. If you use third class, which can take anywhere from six to fifteen days, the end of the first week of the month is a good time to send out your literature. If you use first class, wait until the end of the second week.

OTHER ADVERTISING STRATEGIES

In the last decade, it seems that every available space in the United States has been covered with an ad. There are ads on grocery carts, on the sides of buses, on T-shirts, and on every square inch of most professional athletes. And just when it seems that every idea has been thought of, someone comes up with something new. Frequently, they pass the point of ridiculousness.

Just in the past few months, for example, some enterprising person had the bright idea of putting ads in the bottoms of the cups on golf courses. No, not the cups you drink out of at the water coolers. The ones you putt your ball into on the greens. Thankfully, though, the idea was met with universal derision. Even golfers have *some* dignity.

Still, there are many other forms of advertising that will give you wide exposure, and often for very little expense. Here are a few.

MATCHBOOK COVERS

Although not as popular as they used to be with advertisers, many matchbooks are still covered with ads from mail-order firms. They're particularly effective for products that have a broad appeal. And the inside of the cover can be printed as an order form. Testing matchbook covers can be expensive, though, so it's probably a good idea to wait until your product has proven successful in other media before you try them.

Despite their popularity, the future viability of matchbooks as an advertising vehicle is probably limited. For one thing, many smokers now carry small disposable butane lighters rather than matches. For another, smoking has become such a political issue these days that it might be good public relations to not get too closely associated with it.

On the *other* hand, recent statistics indicate that smoking *is* on the rise among teens. And teens *are* a lucrative market. And many of them *will* use matches. Beyond that, I'll let you make your own conclusions. I don't want to get into an ethical debate.

⑤ "TAKE ONE" ADVERTISING

This is a simple and inexpensive technique that can get your product in front of a lot of people. You have an ad printed on a small sheet of paper and then place a bunch of the small ads in a public place where people can easily grab one.

Sometimes you'll see ads like this on a bus, attached to a larger poster for the mail-order business. They might have a hole punched on one corner, allowing them to hang from a ring attached to the poster (like paper in a three-ring binder). Then when people want to learn more, they simply tear an ad off the ring.

Another way to distribute this type of ad is to have the ads printed in tablet form, kind of like a small legal pad or memo pad. You can then pin the pads to bulletin boards in grocery stores, laundromats, and other public places. People then just peel off an ad if they're interested.

These types of ads reach a large part of the population, so they should only be used for products that have a wide appeal. The products should be fairly inexpensive as well, particularly if you're selling right from the ad. If you're using the inquiry-and-follow-up method, however, you might be able to sell slightly more expensive items.

⑧ Stuffers

Stuffers are advertisements that are "stuffed" into commonly mailed things like packages or bills. You can begin with your own packages. Never send out an order without including a blank order form and additional promotional literature. It's one of the cheapest ways to get exposure, and it's used by mail-order companies of all sizes.

You might also work out an arrangement with another mail-order concern to include your promotional literature in their packages. This can be done in two different ways. One, you pay them a nominal fee for the service. Or two, you agree to stuff their literature in *your* packages. (Just make sure you're not competing with one another.)

Another common arrangement is putting your stuffers in the bills of a large department store. You've probably seen this type of advertising attached to the return envelope of your credit card bills. It's the perforated piece you usually have to tear off before you can seal the envelope. Much as the arrangement with a radio station, you pay the store a certain amount per order generated. You also might send out the merchandise under the name of the store.

⑧ Sunday Newspaper Inserts

If you buy a newspaper each Sunday, I don't have to tell you that most of them contain a lot more advertising than news these days. Mail-order supplements have become big business, and many large metropolitan papers bulge with what seems like several dozen supplements each week. They range from post-

card-sized inquiry-and-follow-up ads to slickly produced eight-
or twelve-page mini-catalogs. Some are from companies that
also have retail outlets, and others are from businesses that
operate strictly by mail order.

There's usually no difference between the promotional materials that companies insert in a newspaper and those they insert
in their own mailings. These companies like newspapers because they're generally a cheaper form of distribution than
third-class postage, and they achieve an approximate market
saturation.

One of the most popular venues for mail-order ads are the
nation's three major Sunday supplements: *Family Weekly, Parade,* and *USA Weekend.* Each week they're full of mail-order
ads for all sorts of items. And because they're targeted for
different markets, you can arrange to have your ad placed only
in those copies that will be distributed in certain cities.

COMIC BOOKS

Never underestimate the marketing power of comic books.
They're read by many children and teens as well as a surprising
number of adults. A lot of mail-order companies that sell novelty products aimed at kids and adolescents have found comic
books to be excellent vehicles for their ads.

COOPERATIVE MAILINGS

Some mail-order companies are fond of putting their promotional literature in the same mailing with that of other companies and sending it off en masse to potential customers. They
do this for one simple reason—it saves money. Using the same
envelope, they can split up the bulk rate costs they would each
pay individually if they did their own mailings.

There are several companies that maintain huge mailing lists
and specialize in putting together "co-op" mailings. Some
charge a flat rate to include your insert (typically around $50
per thousand). Others operate with a "per inquiry" system.
Most co-op mailings fall into one of four categories:

- **Mail-Order Co-op** mailings are sent by a company to its own mailing list. The company then charges participating businesses to include their inserts in the mailing.

- **Magazine Co-op** mailings are sent by magazines using their subscription lists. Participants pay the magazine to have their inserts included.

- **Specialty Co-op** mailings are aimed at certain demographic groups. College students are one example. Young parents are another.

- **Mass Customer Co-op** mailings are general mailings that reach addresses culled from automobile registrations and other lists. The Reuben H. Donnelly/Carol Wright mailings, which you've probably received, are a good example of this type of mailing. They typically send out a half dozen or more mailings to more than 20 million households every year.

WHAT'S NEXT?

Up to this point, we've looked at mail order from a fairly traditional perspective. But the industry is about to change enormously. In fact, I think it's a safe bet that in a few years, many of us will have pretty much stopped using mail order the way we do now. Why? Because we'll be operating in cyberspace—buying and selling goods and services, doing our banking, paying our bills, corresponding with our friends and relatives, attending classes, and maybe even ordering our groceries—while sitting in front of our computers or televisions.

The reason for this is the Internet, the global web of computer networks that's linking millions of people and businesses around the world. In my opinion, it's *the* future of the mail-order industry. In chapter 11, we'll take a look at the Internet and what it means for mail-order businesses.

FOR MORE INFORMATION

These publications are excellent sources for the names of mailing list brokers, advertising agencies, and mail-order firms:

- *Catalog Age* includes a Marketplace section with many classified listings. It's available free to mail-order firms and can be ordered from 125 Elm St., P.O. Box 4006, New Canaan, CT 06840-4006.

- *Direct Marketing* has the most comprehensive advertising section in the industry. It's available in many libraries and can be ordered from 224 Seventh St., Garden City, NY 11530 or by calling 516-746-6700.

- *The Direct Marketing Market Place* lists a variety of suppliers and mail-order firms. It can be ordered from Hilary House, 1033 Channel Drive, Hewlett Harbor, NY 11557.

- *Target Marketing* includes a large classified listing of brokers, advertising agencies, consultants, and other suppliers. You can order a subscription from North American Publishing Company, 401 North Broad St., Philadelphia, PA 19108.

- To keep abreast of the advertising industry, you should subscribe to *Advertising Age*. This publication is the bible of the industry and is published each week. The address is 740 North Rush Street, Chicago, IL 60611.

THE ELECTRONIC STOREFRONT

Earlier in this book, I discusssed the Internet and how it's about to revolutionize the way mail-order businesses operate. I may have made it sound like this revolution is still in the future. It's not. It has already started. There are thousands of businesses on-line, and their numbers are growing every single day.

Some of them are simply using their sites as an electronic version of the inquiry-and-follow-up method. These are usually just a single "page" that describes the business's product or service and includes addresses and phone numbers that customers can contact for more information. Others, however, are the equivalent of a printed catalog, with a full listing and descriptions of products, price lists, and illustrations or photographs of merchandise.

After customers look through these electronic catalogs, they can make purchases in several ways—by sending their order and credit card number via E-mail; by calling the business on a toll-free number and placing an order over the phone; or by printing the order form from their computer, filling it out, and sending it in the mail with a check.

As this book was being written, almost all the mail-order sites found on the Internet were run by small businesses. The nation's premier mail-order operators have been a bit slower to take the dive into cyberspace. This is certainly understandable. For them, creating the electronic equivalent of a sixty-or seventy-page color catalog is a major expense. One study of the industry estimated that it would cost more than $3 million a year to create and maintain a site large enough to offer the electronic equivalent of catalog shopping. So most of the biggies have been waiting to see how things shake out before they make the investment.

Two notable exceptions to this are L. L. Bean, which has had an extensive, nicely designed site up since early 1996 (http://www.llbean.com/), and Land's End (http://www.landsend.com/). J. Crew has a site, but when I checked (http://www.jcrew.com/), it just listed the company's name, address, and toll-free number. You can be sure, however, that they and other major players in the industry are rapidly getting their sites designed and will have them up very soon.

When they do, the face of the mail-order industry will change forever. Many of us will rarely pick up a catalog, opting instead to sit at our computers, log on to the sites of our favorite businesses, and order merchandise with a few strokes of the keyboard. As easy as 800 numbers are, ordering by E-mail is even easier. You never get a busy signal or get put on hold until a customer service representative becomes available. Your order is delivered from your computer to the merchant's computer. There, it's printed out, processed, and your purchases are sent on their way to your doorstep. It's that simple.

Once you own a computer and a modem, setting up an Internet site can be fairly easy and inexpensive. But before we look at the nuts and bolts of operating an electronic storefront, let's look at the Internet itself.

THE ORIGINS OF THE INTERNET

In a sense, the Internet is a big, happy accident. No one envisioned it turning into the monster it has become. It just sort of happened.

The whole thing started out in the sixties as a Department of Defense project called ARPANET. To support military research projects, the department began linking up a number of large mainframe computers around the country. The users agreed to a standard operating protocol that allowed them to communicate with one another.

In the seventies the network began to expand. Many of the institutions working with the military, including a number of the country's biggest corporations and foremost research universities, were involved in other research, and they realized that the network was a wonderful tool for communicating, sharing information, and collaborating on their own projects. In the eighties the introduction of the personal computer and electronic workstation increased the demand even further. People were discovering the vast wealth of information that could be accessed over the giant network. Eventually, as more and more independent networks wanted to come on-line, overloading became a serious issue.

To help solve the problem, the National Science Foundation in 1985 established four supercomputing centers—at Cornell University, the University of Pittsburgh, the University of Illinois, and the University of California at San Diego. They're linked by high-speed lines capable of carrying an extraordinary amount of information. Just as the airports in cities like Atlanta and Chicago act as hubs for major airline routes, these four sites act as hubs for the trillions of bytes of electronic information that whiz around the country every second of every day. Despite their capacities, however, overloading continues to be a problem as more and more individuals and organizations come on-line.

In its earliest days, almost all Internet users were employees of universities, government agencies, and corporations. Back then, cyberspace was the stomping ground of "computer geeks"—bespectacled, junk food–eating, pocket protector–wearing characters who were more at home in front of a monitor than they were in a room full of people. For a long time, the rest of us looked on from afar, slightly bemused and certainly never dreaming that one day we'd be clamoring to come on board.

The Internet was a very exclusive place for quite a while because unless you knew what you were looking for, finding your way around was difficult. There was also a kind of purity and selflessness to the whole endeavor. People freely shared software with one another, and the idea that the Internet might be used for commercial purposes was viewed with horror.

By the early nineties, however, some engineers at a physics lab in Switzerland were adding a new wrinkle to cyberspace that would open it up even further—the World Wide Web. Technically, "the Web," as it's commonly known, is the graphical interface of the Internet. Put more simply, it's that part of the Internet that can transmit images as well as text. For most users, "the Web" has since become synonymous with "the Internet." And it should be, since this is the part of the Internet that virtually all of us use these days.

The arrival of the Web was accompanied by the development of a variety of "browser" software programs for navigating the Web and viewing images. Suddenly, this strange new world began to seem a lot less threatening (and a lot more interesting), and people began to pay attention real quickly. Companies like Prodigy and America Online began using it to provide services to customers who paid a monthly, use-based fee. But even then, subscribers were limited to the companies' offerings. They didn't really enjoy *complete* access to the Internet.

THE INTERNET TODAY

That has since changed. Today, the availability of even better browser programs, such as Netscape, has made finding your way around the Web easier than ever. Most people can obtain a direct connection from a local provider for $15 or $20 a month. The competition has forced the commercial services to provide full access as well. And the idealistic belief that the Internet should never be used for commerce? Well, that's just a dim memory now. The prospect of making money in cyberspace has generated an electronic stampede that makes the California gold rush look like a stroll in the park.

Although there's no agreement on exactly how many people are connected to the Internet, the most reliable estimates put the number at somewhere between 25 and 30 million world-wide. No one knows for sure because there's no way of monitoring the system. In a sense, the whole thing is kind of like a giant electronic cooperative—new networks join and agree to use the standard addressing protocol to send information.

How fast are businesses coming on-line? In early 1996, InterNIC, an organization that maintains Internet addresses, reported that as of December 8, 1995, there were 152,341 commercial Web sites (sites whose electronic addresses contain ".com," like "llbean.com" or "landsend.com"). It also reported there were 2,000 such sites being added each week. Around the same time, Yahoo, a popular site that collects and categorizes Web sites of all descriptions, reported it was receiving 5,000 submissions a week for evaluation and inclusion in its lists.

No one "owns" the Internet or the Web. That would be impossible. But it does have a management of sorts, a group called the Internet Society. It's made up of volunteers who promote global information exchange and establish operating standards. A subgroup, the Internet Architecture Board, acts as a steering committee on addressing protocols and other issues.

These volunteers are going to be very busy people in the coming years. The Internet is growing so rapidly, and being used for so many things, that some observers are calling it the most significant development in human communication since Gutenberg invented the printing press. They just may be right.

AN ON-LINE SUCCESS STORY

When Jim Spitznagel, whom we met in chapter 6, first moved to Ithaca, he planned on opening another traditional compact disc store. But when he started looking at retail space, he found that lease prices were two to three times what he had paid in Pittsburgh.

"I also talked to a lot of shop owners, and they all said the high overheads made it a tough town to run a business in," he

THE 21ST CENTURY ENTREPRENEUR

recalls. "They said you have to be open seven days a week, ten or twelve hours a day. I had done that for eighteen years with my old store and I just didn't feel like living that kind of life again."

Jim still wanted to get back into the music business, so he investigated selling compact discs by mail order. But he wanted to use his money for a comprehensive inventory to ensure fast service, and he was put off by the cost of having a catalog designed, printed, and mailed. That's when he started thinking about the Internet.

Jim did have some experience selling merchandise in cyberspace. During his last couple of years in Pittsburgh, he worked for the Andy Warhol Museum. At first he was hired as a merchandising consultant while the museum was in the planning and construction phase, a task he performed while still running his business. Soon, however, he was offered a permanent job running the museum's store and its mail-order business.

"I'd been thinking about getting out of my business, anyway," he says. "So when they offered me the job I didn't even have to think twice about it. I said yes, put my store up for sale, and three weeks later it was sold."

One of Jim's first tasks at the museum was to purchase and oversee the installation of a computer system. The museum's management also hired a consultant to hook up the museum, including its store, to the Internet.

"That's how I got my first exposure to the Internet," he says. "I was aware of it, but like a lot of people I really didn't know what it was all about. But the first day the museum was open, we got orders from Japan, Germany, and South America. That made a real impression."

After deciding to start an electronic storefront, Jim began researching the Internet and studying other businesses that had set up shop on the Web. Finally, after three months, he was ready to open. On June 1, 1995, he turned on his computer and Jim's Ithaca Music Shop was up and running. Within just a few months, he was filling orders from around the world.

When you visit Jim's business (http://www.jims.com/), you find an eclectic selection of jazz, blues, rock, reggae, folk, and other musical styles that reflect Jim's attitude that he only wants to sell the kind of music he's interested in. As you move through the site, you're accompanied by Dexter, a cartoon beatnik who has served as Jim's logo and alter ego since he ran his store in Pittsburgh. Dexter will direct you to The Hip List, where Jim lists his regular offerings; to The $8.00 List, which includes items being deleted from manufacturers' inventories; and to Dexter Sez, where you can learn about some of the new and offbeat CDs Jim has added to his inventory. You also can request to have your E-mail address added to Jim's mailing list. Once on the list, you'll receive regular electronic updates on new arrivals and special promotions.

Jim operates the business out of his spacious attic, which he converted into an office with white walls and ceilings and black wall-to-wall carpeting. Comfortable chairs dot the room, and the walls are full of photographs taken of Jim with many of the famous musicians he's met during his career. A stereo sits on a rack at one end of the room, and shelves hold the 4,000 or so CDs he keeps in stock. A long desk holds his computer, modem, phone, a combination fax/copier/printer, and piles of catalogs and phone books. Jim presides over his growing electronic empire from a little nook that looks out a dormer window onto the neighborhood street below. He's a happy man.

STARTING YOUR ELECTRONIC STOREFRONT

Jim's Ithaca Music Shop is just one of thousands of businesses thriving on the Web. As we look at the various questions you need to answer to start a business on-line, we'll let him tell us a few things about his own experiences.

How Do I Create a Web Site?

There are two ways. You can hire someone to do it or you can do it yourself.

If you want to hire someone, you probably won't have to look far. The growth of the Web has been accompanied by the creation of all sorts of "Web Service" businesses, including firms that will design your pages and obtain your URL (uniform resource locator, which is just technospeak for your Web site address) and E-mail address for your business. Many graphic design shops have added Web site design services to their offerings. And there are a lot of computer jocks with some design ability who will help you.

The cost will be directly connected to the complexity and size of your site. The simplest approach is a single page that might include your business name, address, phone and fax numbers, and a description of your product or service. Beyond that, the sky's the limit. Graphics are extremely important in enticing people to look at your page, so you also should include your logo and illustrations or photographs of your merchandise. You also should put in a few links to other sites on the Web so your customers can use your site as a jumping-off point to other Web sites (we'll talk about links shortly). Just remember that creating a Web site can be time-consuming. The longer it takes, the more expensive it will be.

After they've gotten you up and running, most Web designers will either work with you periodically to help you keep your site current or teach you how to update your information yourself.

If you want to do it yourself, you'll find that it's a much simpler task than you thought. In fact, it's really quite fun. There are a number of books available that will teach you the basics of HTML (hypertext markup language), which is the basic tool for formatting text on a Web page. On the Web itself, there is also a great deal of free information about creating Web sites.

Depending on your ambition and skill, you can make your site as complex as you care to. The one area you may a have a problem with is graphics. For example, if you want to include photographs of your merchandise, you're going to need a scanner and several different graphics programs which can take an image and put it into an electronic form you can then place on your Web page. These don't come cheaply.

Jim: "I hired a firm in Cambridge, Massachusetts, called Spinners (http://www.spinners.com), which is owned by a bunch of

MIT grads. We agreed on a flat fee, for which they set up my pages, got my URL and E-mail addresses, and taught me enough that I can update the site myself. It worked out great!''

Will I Have to Pay Rent?

No. The best thing about operating on the Web is the fact that it's free. No one owns it, so you don't have to pay registration fees or ''rent'' for your electronic storefront. Your only real costs will be your Internet connection and your phone lines. And once you have your site up and running, your business is just a few keystrokes away from millions of potential customers.

Jim: ''I have a direct connection through Spinners. It costs me $20 a month.''

Will I Keep my Web Site on my Own Computer?

A computer that houses a Web site is known as a ''server,'' and the electronic information that makes up the site itself is kept on the computer's hard disk. Text takes up very little memory on a server. Photographs and other graphics, on the other hand, take up a lot.

Unless you have an enormously powerful computer, you won't keep your site on your own computer at home. There are several reasons. One, your site may take up a lot of memory, if not at first, then certainly down the road as business improves. Two, in order to be in business twenty-four hours a day (this is one of the advantages of the Web, after all), you'd need to keep a phone line open to your computer twenty-four hours a day, and that can get real expensive. And three, if you start doing a lot of business, your computer has to have enough memory to handle many visits, or ''hits,'' to your site at one time.

This is one reason the major players in the mail-order industry have been dragging their feet a bit. Not only do they need an incredible amount of hard disk space for their sites, they must have computers that can deal with tens of thousands of hits every day. The hardware and software required to run such a site of such size represents a major investment.

What you'll need to do is arrange for a local Internet Service Provider (ISP) to keep your site on their computer and act as your server. (Believe me, they'll have enough equipment to rival NASA!) This will cost you a nominal monthly fee. You'll be able to access the server from your own computer with your modem to make changes on your site.

> Jim: "Part of my arrangement with Spinners is they will keep my Web site on their server. So my Web site is in Cambridge and my business is in Ithaca."

HOW POWERFUL A COMPUTER WILL I NEED?

Because your site will be on another computer, you'll basically be using your computer at home to receive orders via E-mail and to respond to them, if necessary. That means that a middle-of-the-road machine will suit you just fine.

> Jim: "I have a computer with 8 megs of RAM and 500 megs of hard disk space. So far, it's been more than adequate."

HOW WILL I RECEIVE ORDERS AND PAYMENTS?

Businesses on the Web receive most of their orders via E-mail, a number by telephone, and a few by regular mail. E-mail and telephone customers use credit cards to pay for their merchandise. Those who mail in their order forms use both personal checks and credit cards.

This has been one of the sticky areas in doing business online. Because of the way information is transported over the Internet, there are valid concerns about the security of credit card numbers as they move between customer to merchant. The problem is being addressed, and it won't be long before adequate security measures are in place.

A major step was taken in February, 1996, when the Microsoft Corporation and Netscape Communications (with a certain amount of goosing from the VISA and MasterCard folks) announced their intention to develop an industry standard technology to protect the security of credit card transactions in cyberspace. At the time of the announcement, plans were that the new standard would be in effect by the end of the year.

Until the proposed standard, or something like it, is implemented, some people may be reluctant to shop via computer. Interestingly, when L. L. Bean opened its Web site, it still required that all orders be placed via its toll-free telephone numbers or by mail. Hopefully, as you read this, the situation with L.L. Bean has changed. If it has, it means that whatever security measures are available have passed muster with one of the nation's premier mail-order companies. That, in turn, should allay the doubts of any remaining skeptics.

> Jim: "I do most of my business with E-mailed credit card numbers. But for people who are uncomfortable sending their numbers electronically, I have a place on my order form where they can indicate they want me to call them to take their number over the phone. I have some customers who will call to place orders. I've also had maybe three customers who printed out the order form and mailed it to me with a check.
>
> "When an order comes in, I E-mail the customer back to let them know I have everything they ordered and that the order will be shipped the next morning. Sometimes, before I ship it, I'll get another message asking me to add another CD or two to the order or to make some special mailing arrangement.
>
> "It's also incredibly easy for me to get the money from credit card orders. My bank came up and installed a program that lets me send all the credit card information electronically to them every day, so there's no paperwork, no forms. They put the money right in my account. I do nothing. It's great!"

Can I Run the Business by Myself?

Sure, up to a point. Operating in cyberspace streamlines the tasks found in running a store, so you can run it by yourself until your volume gets so large you need to hire help. For example, you don't need to wait on customers, not in the traditional sense, anyway. You can go out to lunch or even take the day off and continue to do business. You also don't have to worry about keeping the shelves neat or the floor swept or the windows clean. All this means you have more control over your time.

Eventually, though, the sheer volume of orders and replying to the E-mail of your customers will put sufficient demands on your time that you'll probably welcome some assistance, even if it's just a part-time person to box and ship orders.

Jim: "I can handle things by myself for the moment. But I can't wait to have a staff. That's one of the things I miss from running my store. I'm really used to having people around to bounce ideas off of, and I miss that.

"When my wife comes home from work, we run ideas back and forth, but it's not the same as working with someone and having that interaction, of looking at a problem and saying, 'Yes, we should do this,' and then having that team there to do it. I trust my own judgment, but it's good to get that feedback.

"I also miss the education I used to get from customers. People would come into the store and tell me about a new release or give me the name of some artist I never heard of. Or they'd buy a disc and then come in the next week and say, 'Have you guys listened to that? It's amazing?' Dealing with customers was great that way."

HOW WILL I ADVERTISE?

This has been the big question for many cyberspace merchants. Having 25 or 30 million potential customers is one thing. Letting them know you exist is another thing altogether.

At this point, the most common method of finding out what's available on the Web is to use a "search engine." This is a program that, using a key word or words supplied by the person doing the search, will kick out the names and URLs of Web sites that match up with the key word. For instance, if you were looking for sites that sell compact discs and cassette tapes, you might use "compact disc," "recorded music," "music," "cassettes,'' or some other related term to key your search. Jim and other folks with Web sites selling recorded music desperately hope their names and URLs appear when such searches are made. Netscape has a search engine called Infoseek. Other popular ones are Magellan, Excite, Lycos, Alta Vista, and Yahoo.

As you roam around the Web, you'll also notice that many sites have advertising for other sites. Most pages on the various search engines have the equivalent of little electronic billboards running across the top. You'll also notice the ads are usually for fairly sizable companies. This type of advertising doesn't come cheap.

One strategy you might pursue is to make an arrangement with other Web merchants to create ''links'' to each another. Links are one of the really neat things about the Web, and they're easy to do. For example, on one of your pages, you might set up a list for your customers called ''Other Businesses You Might Like to Visit.'' Then you'd list the sites by name, not URL, and follow the names with a brief description of what the sites offer. When you're making the list, you follow the simple HTML keyboarding instructions to link those sites from your site. The names of the linked sites then appear highlighted in red or blue, with a line underneath them. When a customer clicks on a highlighted and underlined name, that site opens automatically.

Customers will help you, too. People who maintain their own home pages on the Web almost always include a bunch of links to their favorite sites. It's a way of sharing their interests with one another. Over time, as people discover your business, many of them may create a link to your site. Each one is yet another path to your business.

Of course, you can always do a little old-fashioned advertising with some classifieds or display ads. Not all your business will come via the Web, remember, so getting the word out in the real world can't hurt you. After all, people who spend time on the Web still read newspapers. (Jim runs a little ad in the back of the weekly freebie newspaper in my town. It just has the business name and its URL. That's how I found him.)

Jim: ''This was taken care of by Spinners, the firm that created my site. I'm really not sure exactly what they did, but so far

I'm pretty happy with the number of people who have found
me and the ways they've found me.''

WHO WILL I SELL TO?

Once you're on-line, you literally are just a few keystrokes
away from everyone else who's on-line. The Web is growing
exponentially, and it currently reaches more than sixty nations
around the world.

> Jim: "My customers come from everywhere. I've had orders
> from almost every state. Many of them have come from the
> West Coast, including a lot from Seattle. I've also had a lot
> from Texas. In Europe, I've had orders from England, the Neth-
> erlands, and Finland. I've also had orders from South Africa
> and Brazil. I even got an order from China.''

AM I LIMITED TO DOING BUSINESS JUST ON THE WEB?

Of course not. One of the nice things about doing business
electronically is the fact that your pages can be printed by whoever is logged on to your site. At that point, your electronic
catalog becomes a conventional paper catalog that can be circu-
lated among even more people. This is why you need to make
sure customers can order by phone and through the mail as well
as by E-mail. You never know who might want to buy something, how they found out about your business, or how they
might want to pay for your products.

> Jim: "I've had phone orders and even three orders that arrived
> through the mail. I'm also starting to offer delivery within the
> city limits and on the local college campuses.''

WHAT HAPPENS IF MY INTERNET CONNECTION GOES DOWN?

This is an area that's bound to become more contentious as
more and more businesses come on-line. If you contract with

an Internet service provider and, for whatever reason, its equipment goes down for several hours or several days, it's going to prevent you from doing business. The question then becomes, Who's responsible for your lost income?

For most small businesses, a short interruption will probably be of no real consequence. Seasoned Web users are accustomed to finding sites temporarily inaccessible, and they'll more than likely just try again later. But for a huge mail-order firm, any extended downtime could cost thousands of dollars in lost business. This issue will no doubt be hashed out as larger mail-order firms come on-line. I would guess that eventually a new type of business interruption insurance will cover this, although the premiums might be higher than those for a regular storefront business.

> Jim: "I usually get a notice if my connection is going to be down for a few hours. And I haven't had any situations where I was inaccessible for any significant length of time. But you have to remember that this is part of the risk of doing business. If you're running a conventional storefront business, the electricity goes out or the pipes freeze. There will be problems for Internet businesses, too."

What Kind of Overhead Will I Have?

Not much. Like Jim, you should be able to get a direct Internet hookup for $20 or so a month. You may need to have a second phone line run into your home or office to serve as a dedicated line for your modem. Beyond that, you'll have your utility bills. It's hard to find a cheaper way of doing business.

> Jim: "My overhead consists of my Internet hookup, utilities, and phone bill, all of which I can write off. We also have a mortgage, and I can write off part of that because I use part of the house for my business."

How Will I Ship my Merchandise?

The same way any mail-order company ships its merchandise. You can choose from the various classes of mail offered by the post office or you can use one of the shipping services. It's entirely up to you and the speed with which you want to have your merchandise delivered.

If you do use UPS or Federal Express, you'll be happy to know they both have Web sites (http://www.ups.com/index.html and http://www.fedex.com/). You can check rate schedules, delivery options, and best of all, track packages.

> Jim: "I use the post office and ship everything first class. I don't use UPS or Federal Express unless someone asks me to. I charge a flat $3.00 for shipping domestic orders to the lower forty-eight states unless the order is unusually large. In that case, I'll E-mail the customer and say 'Look, this is going to cost a lot more than $3.00 unless I ship it fourth class. Is that okay?' Most of the time, it's fine.
>
> "Overseas, shipping to most of Europe costs the same. Asia and South Africa are much more expensive than anywhere else. But that's all going to become easier because the post office is going to introduce what it calls "Global Priority" mail. It'll be one price anywhere in the world. That'll make companies like mine really happy."

HOW MUCH DO I NEED TO DO THIS?

So what's the bottom line, you ask? First, let's look at the equipment. You'll need a computer, modem, and printer, which you should be able to buy for somewhere between $2,500 and $3,000. Then you'll need to have your site designed and obtain your URL and E-mail address. This is a bit harder to put a dollar figure on.

First of all, are you doing it yourself or hiring someone? If you're doing it yourself, you can't beat the price. If you're hiring someone, I've seen people offering to create Web pages for anywhere from $20 a page to $100 an hour. Niraj S. Shah of Spinners says it would cost from $3,000 to $4,000 to get a fairly simple small business site up and running. You can also spend a lot more, he says, depending on how complex you want to make the site.

So your equipment will run $2,500 to $3,000. Having your

Web site created might cost another $3,500. Your other major expense will be your inventory. Add the three together and you can get a *very* rough estimate of what it might cost to get a bare-bones Web business up and running.

> Jim: "I'd say that between the computer and other equipment, educating myself, having my site designed and set up, and inventory, it cost me around $20,000 to get up and running. And at least half of that was for inventory."

SO WHERE IS ALL THIS GOING?

The headlong rush into cyberspace is an amazing social and economic phenomenon. It's almost impossible to pick up a newspaper or magazine these days without running into a Web- or Internet-related story. It's even inspired its *own* magazines, both the traditional paper variety on the newsstands, and electronic versions on the Web itself.

Is doing business on the Web here to stay? I'm convinced it is. So are millions of other people. And the fact that L. L. Bean has a site is a good indication that the big mail-order houses are convinced as well. Once they're all on-line, things are going to absolutely explode.

As with any new technology or business practice, however, there will be problems. Perhaps the biggest is going to be getting customers accustomed to a new method of buying goods and services. Granted, quite a few people have jumped right on the bandwagon and are quite comfortable shopping in cyberspace. I suspect, however, they're people who are used to working with computers and revel in everything that computers and the Web have to offer.

But then there are people like the close female relative of mine whom I won't identify by name but who is old enough to be my mother. She hasn't even mastered the *automated teller* yet! I can't imagine she'd *ever* be able to deal with buying something with a computer. And this is a woman who really loves to shop!

Another issue is one of haves and have-nots. There is valid concern that the gap between rich and poor is widening in the United Sates. At the moment, part of that gap is defined as who has access to information technology (some wags call these folks the "cognitive elite") and who doesn't. There are millions of people in this country who don't own computers and are completely ignorant of the Web and everything else about the Internet.

And it's not just a matter of economics. Granted, a significant portion of the population lacks the money to get into computers. But a lot of people who do have the means are intimidated by the technology. Many others just aren't interested. All of them, however, are potential customers who are going to be missed unless some way can be found to lure them into cyberspace.

This is where the wonders of capitalism come into play. Never underestimate the ability of entrepreneurs to make their way to your doorstep. If there's money to be made, they'll figure out a way to do it.

Their way was paved on February 8, 1996, when President Clinton signed into law a bill that will shape the future of telecommunications and information technologies in the United States. The law is designed to deregulate the communications industry and make it more competitive. At stake are billions and billions of dollars. Telephone companies, cable providers, and anyone else who cares to enter the fray are scrambling to reshape the way we receive electronic information into our homes. When they're finished, you can bet that access and user-friendliness won't be issues any longer.

Where will all this lead? Directly to your television, more than likely. Home computers may still be the exception rather than the rule, but almost *every* household has a television. Suppose your cable provider begins offering you Internet access along with your cable programming? Or maybe the phone company will give you a better deal. Or maybe the two will collaborate to bring *all* your telecommunications and Internet hookups directly into a box sitting on your television set?

Then what will happen? Maybe you'll end up sitting in front of your television and buying a pair of boots from L. L. Bean or a compact disc from Jim Spitznagel. Or transferring funds from one bank account to another and paying a few bills. Or contacting your grocery store and selecting your purchases from a menu and having them delivered to your home and the bill debited electronically from your checking account to the store's account. Or calling your daughter who's away at college and being able to see each other on your televisions while you chat.

Will any or all of this happen? Some of it already has. Other things no one has even thought of yet will no doubt occur. We're entering remarkable times. The next ten or twenty years are going to be a lot of fun. They're also going to be extremely profitable for those who take advantage of what the Web has to offer.

WHAT'S NEXT?

Whether you're operating your mail-order business in the three-dimensional world, in cyberspace, or in both, you'll need to learn how to process and ship orders, deal with banks, buy advertising, and carry out myriad other tasks. Think of it as the nuts and bolts part of the business. We'll look at all these in chapter 12.

❧12❧

THE NUTS AND BOLTS STUFF

Selecting the right product or service and getting your customers' attention are the two most important tasks in getting any mail-order business off the ground. Once you're *in* business, however, you'll have to be ready to *do* business. That means getting yourself organized for the day-to-day routine of running the show.

This might be considered a fairly mundane part of the whole process, but it's critical that you pay attention and get everything ready to go *before* you place your first ad or send out your first mailing. You'll have enough to keep you busy once the orders start coming in. Your life will be much easier if you've already figured out the nuts and bolts stuff.

PROCESSING YOUR ORDERS

Processing orders quickly and efficiently is vital to the successful management of your mail-order business. You've attracted your customers' attention and convinced them you have a great product at a fair price. They've indicated their trust in you and your product by sending you their money. Now it's up to you to hold up your end of the deal by getting their purchases to them within the promised time frame. It's an activity that will take up a major part of every day. Doing it right requires careful planning.

ACKNOWLEDGING ORDERS

Some mail-order operators immediately send their customers an acknowledgment card or letter upon receipt of an order. There are two schools of thought on this practice. Some think it's absolutely critical to building good customer relations. They feel it creates customer confidence and loyalty, establishes a certain rapport with the customer, and gives their business an air of professionalism. Others think it's a waste of time and money.

Personally, I think if you're able to send the merchandise out immediately upon receipt of an order, such a card isn't really necessary. But if there will be a delay in filling the order, it's an absolute must. I also think it's a good idea if you're selling an expensive item. Even if the customer understands that there will be a four-week delay in getting his merchandise, he'll feel better knowing his check reached its destination. People worry about their mail getting lost, particularly when there's a lot of money involved.

This is one of the many areas in which your computer will come in handy. You can compose an acknowledgment letter and print it on your business letterhead. Then when you send one out, it just takes a second or two to sign it and stick it in an envelope.

FILLING YOUR ORDERS

The speed with which orders are filled (or not filled, as the case may be) has traditionally been consumers' biggest complaint about buying by mail order. Some mail-order businesses are terrible at sending out merchandise. They let orders pile up while they attend to other matters, or they're too cheap to hire temporary personnel to help fill the orders. Their inability to take care of what is such a critical task has always baffled me.

Getting merchandise out should be your highest priority. It requires organization and establishing a routine. The following steps should be followed every day.

Open and sort your mail

You'll be receiving orders for merchandise, returns, inquiries, correspondence, advertising from other businesses, bills of your own, and a variety of other items. Have a place set aside for each category of mail. Some people prefer wall-mounted shelves or boxes. Others develop a filing system. Use whatever works for you.

Sort your orders by method of payment

Put orders accompanied by a check in one group, those with money orders in a second, and those with credit cards in a third. The reason? To make sure you actually get your money.

Orders accompanied by a money order or credit card number are usually not a problem, so you can mail the merchandise right away. Unfortunately, however, you will have to worry about bad checks. Hopefully they'll be few and far between. But until you've been in business for awhile and have developed a feel for how much of a problem this is, you may want to wait until checks have cleared before you mail out those orders. If after a time you find that problems are rare, you may feel comfortable sending orders right out.

In the meantime, put check orders in a daily file to be shipped later. I recommend waiting two weeks. Most checks will clear in that time.

Record your orders

Keep a record of all your orders and their status in either a ledger or computer file.

Transfer new names and addresses to your master list

You should keep a master list of all customers who have ever ordered from you. Over time, this will become a valuable mailing list. You should enter the names and addresses from that day's orders in your file every day. If an order is from a customer who has done business with you before, double-check to see if the address has changed. If it has, change the address in your master list.

Prepare the orders for shipment

Wrap and box the merchandise, print mailing labels, attach postage, and otherwise prepare orders for shipment. This will include all the money order and credit card orders that arrived during the day as well as the check orders that arrived two weeks previously. Don't forget to include your product literature and an order form. If you drop ship your merchandise, make a record of each order and then forward the orders to the distributor.

Answer other correspondence

Respond to inquiries, resolve problems with returned merchandise (including writing out refund checks, if necessary), and deal with any other mail that must be answered.

Ship the orders

If you use the U.S. mail, you may have to make a daily trip to the post office to ship your orders. (Jim Spitznagel walks to the post office every day to mail his. It's about a half mile each way, down and then back up a steep hill. He says it's great exercise.) If you use UPS or Federal Express, you can call for pickup or arrange to be included on a daily route.

Follow this routine every single day. Otherwise, you'll soon find yourself getting further and further behind in dealing with your orders. If you allow that to happen, it won't be long before you start losing customers.

THE DROP SHIP ARRANGEMENT

We discussed drop shipping briefly in chapter 6. This is when the manufacturer or distributor of your product agrees to stock and ship the product for you. This means you don't have to worry about maintaining inventory or go schlepping down to the post office every day. In a sense, you're almost acting as a broker.

Drop shipping has both advantages and disadvantages. The biggest advantage is you don't need a lot of capital. When you get an order, the customer's check goes right into your account and you write a check to the drop shipper for the merchandise. The difference in the amount of the two checks is your profit.

Another advantage is you don't need inventory space. When you get an order, you simply forward it to the drop shipper with payment and an address label, and he does the rest.

The downside to drop shipping is very few companies offer it, and those that do almost always sell expensive merchandise. They also usually charge more for their merchandise, since they're the ones tying up their capital and storage space.

Another problem is the lack of control you have over when the merchandise is actually shipped. If a drop shipper doesn't follow up on the orders you send him with reasonable speed, there are going to be some very unhappy customers to deal with. And you, not he, will be the person who has to deal with them.

DEALING WITH UNHAPPY CUSTOMERS

Speaking of unhappy customers, you should know that they're just as common in mail order as they are in conventional retail businesses. The only advantage to mail order is that you don't have to deal with them face-to-face.

Still, this doesn't mean you need to be any less courteous to them. If you're communicating by mail, make sure your letters are timely and written in a professional manner. If you speak on the phone, be polite and understanding. Getting irritated or losing your temper will only hurt you in the long run. If a customer requests a refund, agree without argument. To do otherwise is to lose a customer forever. And human nature being what it is, that dissatisfied customer will no doubt complain about you to other people and cost you their business as well.

RECORD KEEPING

Good order fulfillment requires good record keeping. It's not a difficult task. However, it can be time-consuming. You need to keep track of:

1. **Date the order was received.** Enter this immediately after sorting and opening the mail each day. It's critical that the

date be correct if you are going to meet your promised delivery deadline.

2. **Customer's name and address.** Enter this information in your master customer list. Update any address changes of prior customers.

3. **Item(s) ordered.** Include the quantity and name of each item in the order.

4. **Total price.** This is the combined price of all the items in the order.

5. **Amount enclosed with order.** Hopefully this will be the same amount as the amount of the order.

6. **Method of payment.** Check, money order, or credit card. Be sure to also include the number of the check, money order, or card.

7. **Date the order was filled.** This lets you know you met your deadline. It's also important information if the package should disappear en route to the customer.

8. **Shipping cost.** This is particularly important. Postage and shipping are business expenses and will be deducted from your gross sales. This will serve as one record. The receipts from the post office or shipping companies will be others.

9. **Key code.** This will tell you which of your ads generated the order.

You can either create a modified ledger page to record this information, or you can use a computer spreadsheet program. Enter and update the information every day after you've sorted your new orders and sent out that day's merchandise.

You also should create three files for the orders themselves. One will be for orders waiting to be filled (particularly those paid for by check), the second for orders already filled, and the third for ''problem'' orders that require special attention. On the first day of every month, take the orders filled during the previous month and put them in an inactive file. After a few months, you can throw them out. You'll still have the computer record of the transactions should any questions arise down the road. Those, too, can periodically be archived onto floppy disks if you need more space on your computer's hard disk.

You can't be too detailed with your record keeping, so this is the perfect task for someone with an obsessive personality. But if you're someone whose approach to paperwork is a bit more, shall we say, "loosey goosey," you may need to make a concerted effort to stay on top of things. The idea is that you should be able to turn on your computer, look at your records, and know the current status of every order you've received.

INVENTORY CONTROL

In chapter 4 I included maintaining minimal inventory as one of the 12 Rules For Doing It Cheaply. This is because inventory requires money, and the more inventory you keep on hand, the more money you'll need. It can represent 15 to 25 percent of your total operating capital.

The key to minimizing your inventory—and your capital investment—is having a good inventory control system in place. As I pointed out in chapter 4, you need to look at inventory in terms of the capital it represents. Having inventory sitting idly on your shelves is just like having your money sitting there twiddling its thumbs when it could be doing something really useful like earning interest.

The key to inventory control is accurately timing your purchases from suppliers with the receipt of your customers' orders. In a perfect world, your inventory will be sent on its way to your customers the moment it arrives from your suppliers. This is called "turning over" inventory, and the faster you can accomplish it, the better off you'll be. Unfortunately, we don't live in a perfect world. But once you learn to time your purchases to keep just enough inventory on hand to fill orders, you'll find that things are pretty darn nice.

Using Time to Your Advantage

One of the great things about the mail-order business is that, unlike a retail storefront, you don't always need to have merchandise on hand to make a sale. You just need to be able to get it to your customers within the promised time frame. The best example of this is the drop ship arrangement.

The shorter the time frame for delivery, the greater the need to keep inventory on hand. For example, if you promise shipment immediately or even within a week or two of receipt of an order, you'd better have the merchandise sitting there when the order arrives. If, on the other hand, your customers expect to wait four to six weeks for their purchases to arrive, you may be able to wait until you've amassed a week's worth of orders before you purchase the merchandise needed to fill them. You've already been paid for the merchandise by your customers. When it arrives, you ship it right out to them. It's about as fast an inventory turnover as you could ask for.

The key to this, as you've no doubt guessed, is finding a supplier or suppliers who can guarantee, and I mean *guarantee,* shipment of your merchandise in time for you to fulfill your own delivery commitments to your customers. (As you'll see later in this chapter, there are strict Federal Trade Commission regulations regarding timely delivery of merchandise. They're not to be fooled with.)

The faster you can get merchandise from a supplier, the more options you'll have in filling your orders. For example, if you have a reliable supplier who can promise delivery within a week to ten days, and you promise delivery to your customers within four to six weeks, you *can* wait until you have a week's worth of orders before you purchase the inventory to fill them. When the merchandise arrives, you'll still have plenty of time to get it to your customers within the promised time frame.

Having said all this, I'll also point out that juggling orders and inventory in this manner can be hard to do. First of all, depending on what you're selling and the type of people you're selling to, a four- to six-week wait may just not be acceptable. This will certainly be the case if they can get the same item more quickly from someone else. And finding suppliers who can get merchandise to you in the requisite time frame is not always possible. Nevertheless, if you can find the right product and the right suppliers, it's a great way to do business.

SHIPPING YOUR ORDERS

You can use the U.S. Postal Service or one of the package delivery services like UPS or Federal Express to ship your orders. Which you use depends on what you're shipping, how fast you want it to get to your customers, and how much you want to spend. Many of the big mail-order houses like L. L. Bean and Land's End have contractual relationships with one or more delivery services. Most small mail-order firms, however, use the post office for their routine, day-to-day business.

USING THE U.S. POSTAL SERVICE

Perhaps the most ridiculed branch of the federal government, the U.S. Postal Service has in fact improved its service remarkably in recent years. Considering the sheer volume of stuff it has to move around the country, it really does a pretty darn good job. The USPS offers mail-order businesses a wide variety of mailing services.

- **Express Mail** guarantees overnight delivery for letters and packages up to a certain size and weight. It's expensive, but it's a great solution for a situation in which a customer needs an item immediately.

- **Priority Mail** offers expedited delivery of first-class mail when overnight delivery isn't necessary. Most priority mail is deliverable in two days.

- **First-class Mail** is the standard method for delivering correspondence, bills, postcards, and other packages weighing less than 11 ounces. First-class mail weighing more than 11 ounces is automatically treated as priority mail.

- **Second-class Mail** is reserved for the publishers of newspapers, magazines, and other periodicals that are sold by subscription.

- **Third-class Mail** is most commonly used by businesses and organizations who take advantage of bulk mail discounts that apply to mailings of 200 or more addressed

pieces (usually printed matter) or 50 pounds or more of
addressed pieces (usually packages or a mixture of printed
matter and packages). It includes advertising mailings, merchandise, and other materials weighing less than a pound.
It excludes letters, bills, statements of account, and checks.
These must be sent first class.

Third-class mail is how most mail-order businesses send
out their promotional literature and catalogs. There are various requirements for bulk rate mailings and an annual
presort fee that must be paid to the post office where the
mailings are made. Postage may be paid by permit imprints
that are printed in the address area of the literature, provided a permit is on file with the post office where the
mailings are made.

- **Fourth-class Mail,** which includes parcel post, is for mailing packages, merchandise, and printed matter weighing
  more than a pound. Delivery can vary from two to seven
  days or more, depending on distance.

- **Business Reply Mail** allows you to send your customers
  preaddressed, prepaid postcards and envelopes for their orders or inquiries. You only pay for the postage on the ones
  that are actually returned to you. It saves the customer the
  hassle of filling out your address and sticking on a stamp.

POSTAL BUSINESS CENTERS

The USPS maintains nearly 100 postal business centers around the
country to provide basic customer service to business mailers. Their
services range from answering questions over the phone to providing assistance in designing a mail piece. Other services include:

- establishing corporate accounts for Express Mail;
- information on mailing list management and services;
- mailing preparation;

- information on obtaining permits;
- obtaining mailing supplies (trays, sacks, Express Mail and Priority Mail envelopes and labels, stickers, rubber bands, etc.); and
- postal publications and next-step help.

Here are the addresses, phone numbers, and fax numbers of the postal business centers in each state:

ALABAMA

351 24th St. N
Birmingham, AL 35203-6961
(205) 323-6510
(205) 521-0046 (fax)
ZIPS served: 350-352, 354-368

ALASKA

3201 C Street, Suite 505
Anchorage, AK 99503-9996
(907) 564-2823
(907) 564-2882 (fax)
ZIPS served: 995-999

ARIZONA

4949 East Van Buren St., Rm. 8
Phoenix, AZ 85026-9605
(602) 225-5454
(602) 225-5432 (fax)
ZIPS served: 850, 852-853, 855, 859-860, 863-864

1501 S. Cherrybell Strav.
Tucson, AZ 85726-9605
(602) 620-5108
(602) 620-5121 (fax)
ZIPS served: 856-857

ARKANSAS

420 Natural Resources Dr.
Little Rock, AR 72205-9996
(501) 228-4304
(501) 228-4299 (fax)
ZIPS served: 716-729

CALIFORNIA

2300 Redondo Ave.
Long Beach, CA 90809-9694
(310) 494-2301
(310) 498-7506 (fax)
ZIPS served: 902-908

7001 S. Central Ave., Rm. 264
Los Angeles, CA 90052-9602
(213) 586-1843
(213) 586-1831 (fax)
ZIPS served: 900

1675 7th St., Rm. 120
Oakland, CA 94615-9641
(510) 874-8600
(510) 832-4124 (fax)
ZIPS served: 945-948

2035 Hurley Way, Suite 200
Sacramento, CA 95825-3209
(916) 923-4357
(916) 923-4381 (fax)
ZIPS served: 942, 952, 953, 956-960

11251 Rancho Carmel Dr., Rm. 266
San Diego, CA 92199-9606
(619) 674-0400
(619) 674-0055 (fax)
ZIPS served: 919-925

PO Box 193000
San Francisco, CA 94119-3000
(415) 550-6565
(415) 285-0253 (fax)
ZIPS served: 940-941, 943-944,
949, 954-955, 962-966

PO Box 50014
San Jose, CA 95150-0014
(408) 723-6262
(408) 723-6272 (fax)
ZIPS served: 932-933, 936-939,
950-951

3101 W. Sunflower Ave.
Santa Ana, CA 92799-9323
(714) 662-6213
(714) 556-1492 (fax)
ZIPS served: 917-918, 926-928

15701 Sherman Way
Van Nuys, CA 91409-9680
(818) 374-4943
ZIPS served: 910-916, 929-931,
934-935

COLORADO

1745 Stout St., Suite 101
Denver, CO 80266-9617
(303) 297-6118
(303) 391-5076 (fax)
ZIPS served: 800-816, 820-831

CONNECTICUT

141 Weston St.
Hartford, CT 06101-9631
(203) 524-6446
ZIPS served: 060-069

DISTRICT OF COLUMBIA

8455 Colesville Rd., Suite 950
Silver Spring, MD 20910-3319
(301) 565-2177
(301) 565-2933 (fax)
ZIPS served: 200, 202-209

FLORIDA

1900 W. Oakland Park Blvd.
Fort Lauderdale, FL 33310-9699
(305) 527-6981
(305) 527-9600 (fax)
ZIPS served: 333

11250 Phillips Industrial Blvd. E.
Jacksonville, FL 32256-3000
(904) 260-8101
(904) 260-9015 (fax)
ZIPS served: 320-326, 344

200 NW 72nd Ave., Rm. 528
Miami, FL 33152-9600
(305) 470-0803
(305) 470-0799 (fax)
ZIPS served: 330-332, 340

10401 Tradeport Dr.
Orlando, FL 32862-8901
(407) 826-5602
(407) 826-5679 (fax)
ZIPS served: 327-329, 347

4107 N. Himes Ave., Suite 203
Tampa, FL 33607-6600
(813) 871-6245
(813) 871-2021 (fax)
ZIPS served: 335-339, 342, 346

3200 Summit Blvd.,
Rm. 111
West Palm Beach, FL 33406-9602
(407) 697-2180
(407) 697-2125 (fax)
ZIPS served: 334, 349

GEORGIA

PO Box 20777
Macon, GA 31213-0777
(912) 784-3917
(912) 784-3916 (fax)
ZIPS served: 310, 312, 316-319

PO Box 599332
North Metro, GA 30159-9332
(404) 717-3440
(404) 717-3629 (fax)
ZIPS served: 300-303, 305-306,
311

2 N. Fahm St.
Savannah, GA 31402-9600
(912) 235-4591
(912) 234-9335 (fax)
ZIPS served: 298-299, 304,
308-309, 313-315

HAWAII

3600 Aolele St.
Honolulu, HI 96820-9623
(808) 423-3761
(808) 423-3708 (fax)
ZIPS served: 967-969

ILLINOIS

3900 Gabrielle Lane
Aurora, IL 60599-9610
(708) 978-4455
(708) 978-4354 (fax)
ZIPS served: 604-605, 609, 613-
619, 625-627

500 E. Fullerton Ave.
Carol Stream, IL 60199-9661
(708) 260-5511
(708) 260-5524 (fax)
ZIPS served: 600-603, 610-611

433 W. Van Buren St., Rm. 108
Chicago, IL 60607-9601
(312) 765-4215
(312) 765-3984 (fax)
ZIPS served: 606-607

INDIANA

125 W. South St.
Indianapolis, IN 46206-9661
(317) 464-6010
(317) 464-6266 (fax)
ZIPS served: 460-469, 472-475,
478-479

IOWA

PO Box 189996
Des Moines, IA 50318-9605
(515) 251-2336
(515) 251-2052 (fax)
ZIPS served: 500-514, 520-528,
612

KENTUCKY

PO Box 31660
Louisville, KY 40231-9660
(502) 473-4200
(502) 454-1744 (fax)
ZIPS served: 400-409, 411-418,
420-427, 471, 476-477

LOUISIANA

701 Loyola Ave., Rm. 1003
New Orleans, LA 70113-9680
(504) 589-1366
(504) 589-1328 (fax)
ZIPS served: 700-701, 703-708,
710-714

MAINE

125 Forest Ave.
Portland, ME 04101-9600
(207) 871-8567
(207) 871-8401 (fax)
ZIPS served: 039-049

MARYLAND

900 E. Fayette St., Rm. 502
Baltimore, MD 21233-9661
(410) 347-4358
(410) 347-4515 (fax)
ZIPS served: 210-212, 214-219

MASSACHUSETTS

25 Dorchester Ave., Rm. 1000
Boston, MA 02205-9602
(617) 654-5725
(617) 654-5829 (fax)
ZIPS served: 021-022

1883 Main St.
Springfield, MA 01101-9600
(413) 731-0306
(413) 731-0330 (fax)
ZIPS served: 010-013, 050-059

PO Box 2236
Woburn, MA 01888-0338
(617) 938-1450
(617) 938-5827 (fax)
ZIPS served: 018-019, 01730,
01741, 01742

4 East Central St.
Worcester, MA 01613-9602
(508) 795-3608
(508) 795-3660 (fax)
ZIPS served: 014-017

MICHIGAN

PO Box 9630
Birmingham, MI 48009-9630
(810) 546-1321
(313) 901-4515 (fax)
ZIPS served: 480, 483

1927 Rosa Parks Blvd.
Detroit, MI 48216-9620
(313) 225-5445
(313) 961-1979 (fax)
ZIPS served: 481-482

PO Box 999661
Grand Rapids, MI 49599-9661
(616) 776-6161
(616) 458-5830 (fax)
ZIPS served: 484-497

MINNESOTA

100 S. First St., Rm. 119
Minneapolis, MN 55401-9617
(612) 349-6360
(612) 349-4410 (fax)
ZIPS served: 540. 546-548,
550-551, 553-564, 566

MISSISSIPPI

401 E. South St., Suite 100
Jackson, MS 39201-9825
(601) 360-2700
(601) 360-2702 (fax)
ZIPS served: 369, 386-397

MISSOURI

315 W. Pershing Rd., Rm. 104
Kansas City, MO 64108-9623
(816) 374-9513
(816) 374-9192 (fax)
ZIPS served: 636-641, 644-649,
654-658, 660-662, 667

2665 Scott Ave.
St. Louis, MO 63103-3048
(314) 534-2678
(314) 534-4763 (fax)
ZIPS served: 620, 622-624, 628-
631, 633-635, 650-653

MONTANA

550 S. 24th St. W.
Billings, MT 59102-6293
(406) 255-6432
(406) 255-6433 (fax)
ZIPS served: 590-595, 59715

110 W. Kent Ave.
Missoula, MT 59801-9625
(406) 329-2231
(406) 329-2280 (fax)
ZIPS served: 596-599

NEBRASKA

5303 N. 91st Ave.
Omaha, NE 68134-9600
(402) 573-2100
(402) 573-2131 (fax)
ZIPS served: 515-516, 664-666,
668-681, 683-693

NEVADA

1001 E. Sunset Rd.
Las Vegas, NV 89199-9605
(702) 361-9318
(702) 361-9213 (fax)
ZIPS served: 889-891, 893-895,
897-898, 961

NEW HAMPSHIRE

955 Goffs Falls Rd.
Manchester, NH 03103-9671
(603) 644-3838
(603) 644-3865 (fax)
ZIPS served: 030-038

NEW JERSEY

PO Box 9001
Bellmawr, NJ 08099-9996
(609) 933-6000
(609) 933-6006 (fax)
ZIPS served: 080-084, 197-199

21 Kilmer Rd.
Edison, NJ 08899-9610
(908) 777-0565
(908) 777-0513 (fax)
ZIPS served: 077-079, 085-089

100 Executive Dr., Suite 390
West Orange, NJ 07052-9331
(201) 731-4866
(201) 669-0489 (fax)
ZIPS served: 070-076

NEW MEXICO

1135 Broadway Blvd. NE,
Room 108
Albuquerque, NM 87101-9601
(505) 245-9480
(505) 245-9804 (fax)
ZIPS served: 865, 870-875, 877-884

NEW YORK

1770 Central Ave.
Albany, NY 12205-4753
(518) 869-6526
(518) 869-3925 (fax)
ZIPS served: 120-123, 128-139

1200 Williams St., Rm. 100
Buffalo, NY 14240-9661
(716) 846-2581
(716) 846-2586 (fax)
ZIPS served: 140-143, 147

500 N. Saw Mill River Rd.
Elmsford, NY 10523-9650
(914) 345-1237
(914) 345-3451 (fax)
ZIPS served: 105-109, 124-127

14202 20th Ave., Rm. 122
Flushing, NY 11351-9621
(718) 321-5700
(718) 358-9196 (fax)
ZIPS served: 103, 110-114, 116

PO Box 7609
Hauppauge, NY 11760-9661
(516) 582-7600
(516) 582-7596 (fax)
ZIPS served: 115, 117-119

421 8th Ave., Rm. 4202H
New York, NY 10199-9619
(212) 330-2824
(212) 330-3801 (fax)
ZIPS served: 100-102, 104

PO Box 22908
Rochester, NY 14692-5979
(716) 272-7220
(716) 272-5979 (fax)
ZIPS served: 144-146, 148-149

NORTH CAROLINA

2901 I-85 S. Service Rd.
Charlotte, NC 28228-9975
(704) 393-4427
(704) 393-4661 (fax)
ZIPS served: 280-285,
287-289, 297

PO Box 27499
Greensboro, NC 27498-9661
(910) 665-9740
(910) 665-9741 (fax)
ZIPS served: 270-279, 286

OHIO

675 Wolf Ledges Pkwy.
Akron, OH 44309-9600
(216) 996-9721
(216) 996-9948 (fax)
ZIPS served: 434-436, 439, 442-449

990 Dalton Ave.
Cincinnati, OH 45203-9601
(513) 723-9900
(513) 684-5082 (fax)
ZIPS served: 410, 450-455,
458, 470

2400 Orange Ave., Rm. 23
Cleveland, OH 44101-9604
(216) 443-4401
(216) 443-4410 (fax)
ZIPS served: 440-441

850 Twin Rivers Dr.
Columbus, OH 43216-9601
(614) 469-4336
(614) 469-4417 (fax)
ZIPS served: 430-433,
437-438, 456-457

OKLAHOMA

7101 NW Expressway St.
Suite 325
Oklahoma City, OK 73132-1598
(405) 720-2675
(405) 720-7120 (fax)
ZIPS served: 730-731,
734-741, 743-749

OREGON

PO Box 4029
Portland, OR 97208-4029
(503) 294-2306
(503) 294-2304 (fax)
ZIPS served: 970-979, 986

PENNSYLVANIA

1314 Griswold Plaza
Erie, PA 16501-9631
(814) 878-0002
(814) 878-0010 (fax)
ZIPS served: 155, 157-168

1425 Crooked Hill Rd.
Harrisburg, PA 17107-9601
(717) 257-2108
(717) 257-2101 (fax)
ZIPS served: 169-172,
177-178, 180-188

1400 Harrisburg Pike
Lancaster, PA 17604-9601
(717) 396-6994
(717) 295-7525 (fax)
ZIPS served: 173-176, 179, 195-196

PO Box 13416
Philadelphia, PA 19101-3416
(215) 895-8046
(215) 895-8041 (fax)
ZIPS served: 190-192

1001 California Ave., Rm. 1007
Pittsburgh, PA 15290-9652
(412) 359-7601
(412) 321-1953 (fax)
ZIPS served: 150-156, 260

1000 W. Valley Rd.
Southeastern, PA 19399-9604
(215) 964-6441
(215) 964-5414 (fax)
ZIPS served: 189, 193-194

PUERTO RICO

585 F.D.R. Ave., Suite 216
San Juan, PR 00936-9623
(809) 782-3929
(809) 273-1025 (fax)
ZIPS served: 006-009

RHODE ISLAND

24 Corliss St.
Providence, RI 02904-9602
(401) 276-5038
(401) 276-5089 (fax)
ZIPS served: 020, 023-029

SOUTH CAROLINA

PO Box 929642
Columbia, SC 29292-9642
(803) 926-6332
(803) 926-6470 (fax)
ZIPS served: 290-296

SOUTH DAKOTA

320 S. 2nd Ave.
Sioux Falls, SD 57102-7574
(605) 339-8854
(605) 335-3864 (fax)
ZIPS served: 565, 567, 57-577, 580-588

TENNESSEE

PO Box 3463
Memphis, TN 38173-0463
(901) 576-2035
(901) 576-2039 (fax)
ZIPS served: 380-383

525 Royal Pkwy., Rm. 327
Nashville, TN 37229-9601
(615) 885-9399
(615) 885-9214 (fax)
ZIPS served: 307, 370-374, 376-379, 384-385

TEXAS

951 W. Bethel Rd.
Coppell, TX 75099-9681
(214) 393-6701
(214) 393-6770 (fax)
ZIPS served: 750-759

4600 Mark IV Pkwy.,
Suite 260K
Fort Worth, TX 76161-9681
(817) 625-3600
(817) 625-3304 (fax)
ZIPS served: 739, 760-764, 768-769, 790-796

PO Box 250001
Houston, TX 77202-9610
(713) 226-3349
(713) 226-3155 (fax)
ZIPS served: 770-778

4600 Aldine Bender Rd., Rm. 227
Houston, TX 77315-9610
(713) 985-4108
(713) 985-4194 (fax)
ZIPS served: 770-778

10410 Perrin Beitel Rd., Rm. 1069
San Antonio, TX 78284-9623
(210) 657-8578
(210) 657-8463 (fax)
ZIPS served: 733, 765-767, 779-789, 797-799

UTAH

1760 W. 2100 St.
Salt Lake City, UT 84199-9625
(801) 974-2503
(801) 975-7886 (fax)
ZIPS served: 840-841, 843-847

VERMONT

Vermont is served by the Postal
Business Center in Springfield, MA.
Call 1-800-230-2370

VIRGINIA

8409 Lee Hwy., Rm. 1-8
Merrifield, VA 22081-9621
(703) 207-6800
(703) 207-6825 (fax)
ZIPS served: 201, 220-223, 226-227

1801 Brook Rd.
Richmond, VA 23232-9610
(804) 775-6224
(804) 775-6287 (fax)
ZIPS served: 224-225, 228-239, 244

WASHINGTON

PO Box 24000
Seattle, WA 98124-4000
(206) 635-7016
(206) 467-9019 (fax)
ZIPS served: 980-985, 988-989

707 West Main Ave.,
Suite 600
Spokane, WA 99299-9641
(509) 626-6733
(509) 626-6918 (fax)
ZIPS served: 832-838, 990-994

WEST VIRGINIA

PO Box 59661
Charleston, WV 25350-9661
(304) 340-4233
(304) 340-2709 (fax)
ZIPS served: 240-243, 245-259, 261-268

WISCONSIN

PO Box 14750
Madison, WI 53714-0750
(608) 246-1245
(608) 246-1258 (fax)
ZIPS served: 535-539, 549

PO Box 5008
Milwaukee, WI 53201-5008
(414) 287-2522
(414) 287-2518 (fax)
ZIPS served: 498-499, 530-532, 534-535, 537-539, 541-545, 549, 362, 368

USPS PUBLICATIONS

The USPS also publishes a number of publications you might find helpful in running your mail-order business.

Address Information Systems (Publication 40)—A guide to products to improve the quality of your address files. Available free from your post office or postal business center.

Addressing for Success (Notice 221)—A guide to addressing for compatibility with automated processing equipment. Available free from your post office or postal business center.

Business Reply Mail Accounting System (Notice 46)—Describes a system to reduce costs for business reply mail users. Available free from your post office or postal business center.

Designing Business Letter Mail (Publication 25)—A technical guide to designing letter mail for automation. Includes guidelines for machinability, readability, and barcoding. Available free from your post office or postal business center.

Designing Flat Mail (Publication 63)—A guide to designing flat mail to meet machinability and readability requirements. Includes information on mailpiece design, address format and location, and barcoding. Available free from your post office or postal business center.

Designing Reply Mail (Publication 353)—Outlines the formats, features, and technical specifications for designing envelopes and cards for business reply use. Available free from your post office or postal business center.

Domestic Mail Manual—The office manual of postal service regulations, procedures, and services. Available by paid subscription from Superintendent of Documents, U.S. Government Printing Office, 710 N. Capitol St., NW, Washington, D.C. 20402-9325.

Metering (Notice 125)—A pamphlet on how to use postage meters. Includes tips on proper metering. Available free from your post office or postal business center.

National ZIP Code Directory—Lists zip codes for every mailing address in the United States. Purchase from Superintendent of Documents, U.S. Government Printing Office, 710 N. Capitol St., NW, Washington, D.C. 20402-9325.

Postal Addressing Standards (Publication 28)—Provides guidelines on addressing format standards and options. Available free from your post office or postal business center.

Third-Class Mail Preparation (Publication 49)—Describes third-class bulk business mail including rate categories, payment options, sorting, and filling out forms. Available free from your post office or postal business center.

Postal Abbreviations

These are the designated USPS abbreviations for all U.S. states and territories.

Alabama	AL	Kentucky	KY
Alaska	AK	Louisiana	LA
American Samoa	AS	Maine	ME
Arizona	AZ	Marshall Islands	MH
Arkansas	AR	Maryland	MD
California	CA	Massachusetts	MA
Colorado	CO	Michigan	MI
Connecticut	CT	Minnesota	MN
Delaware	DE	Mississippi	MS
District of Columbia	DC	Missouri	MO
Federated States of		Montana	MT
Micronesia	FM	Nebraska	NE
Florida	FL	Nevada	NV
Georgia	GA	New Hampshire	NH
Guam	GU	New Jersey	NJ
Hawaii	HI	New Mexico	NM
Idaho	ID	New York	NY
Illinois	IL	North Carolina	NC
Indiana	IN	North Dakota	ND
Iowa	IA	Northern Mariana	
Kansas	KS	Islands	MP

Ohio	OH	Texas	TX
Oklahoma	OK	Utah	UT
Oregon	OR	Vermont	VT
Palau	PW	Virgin Islands	VI
Pennsylvania	PA	Virginia	VA
Puerto Rico	PR	Washington	WA
Rhode Island	RI	West Virginia	WV
South Carolina	SC	Wisconsin	WI
South Dakota	SD	Wyoming	WY
Tennessee	TN		

SHOULD YOU USE A SHIPPING SERVICE?

Sure, if its rates are cheaper than those of the USPS for the particular type of package you're shipping. And if you have a package that exceeds the size or weight limits of the post office, you'll *have* to use a shipping service. You should determine your shipping needs while you're getting your business organized. Compare the post office's rates and delivery schedules with those of the various services. Also determine if there will be special situations in which a shipping service will be preferable to the post office.

FOLLOWING THE RULES

Now that you've learned just how lucrative mail order can be, it shouldn't come as a surprise to learn that there are a lot of charlatans and get-rich-quick artists in the industry working all sorts of scams. It's nothing new. Mail order has always attracted more than its share of crooks.

In the early days, shady mail-order operators would either fail to send the merchandise that was ordered, or they would send merchandise of considerably less quality than what they had advertised. Over time, the enactment of new laws helped protect consumers against many of these practices. Still, failure to receive merchandise remains the number one complaint of consumers against mail-order businesses.

Other common complaints are orders that are only partially filled, merchandise that arrives damaged, merchandise that doesn't work as advertised or is otherwise unsatisfactory, and money-back guarantees that aren't honored. And despite the best efforts of the industry and those who regulate it, the number of complaints continues to rise every year.

Mail-order fraud now costs American consumers more than $500 million every year. Read this section carefully. It will help protect you as well as your customers.

ILLEGAL MAIL-ORDER ACTIVITIES

The boundaries of mail order are constantly being tested by people whose ethics and honesty are somewhat shaky. Over the years, all sorts of schemes have been tried, and just about every product imaginable has been sold. Many of these practices will attract the attention of the postal inspector. A few have been deemed illegal.

Pyramid schemes

These have always been a thorn in the side of the industry. Depending on the way they're structured, some manage to skirt the edges of the law. The one type of pyramid scheme that's easy to spot and is almost always illegal is based on the chain letter concept. This is a deal in which you're supposed to send something to all the people on a list you receive in the mail. This act supposedly puts you on the lists received by many other people, all of whom will be sending you something, deluging you in whatever the item happens to be. I've seen it done with books, compact discs, golf shirts, recipes, and even one-dollar bills.

Pornography and other "obscene" materials

Selling through the mail pornography and other material that might be deemed "obscene" is illegal. It's an area that arouses great public indignation and the attention of many zealous prosecutors, so these laws should not be taken lightly.

Recently, as more and more people have begun shopping on the Web, debate has arisen over a whole new issue—pornography in cyberspace. The communications bill signed by President Clinton took a broad swipe at the question that left many civil libertarians aghast. A lot more work needs to be done to determine just how the whole thing will be handled.

Lotteries

Selling any gambling scheme via mail order is illegal. This area also covers many "games" that upon closer inspection are really just forms of gambling.

FALSE ADVERTISING

False advertising is just what it says. Mail-order regulators frown upon hyperbole. If you run an ad that makes any false or even "excessive" claims about the virtues or abilities of your product, you could be in violation of the law.

This is an area where a lot of people get into trouble because of their own enthusiasm. They never would dream of trying to rip someone off, but in their excitement over their product, they get a bit carried away in their advertising. The next thing they know, the postal inspector is at their door.

The best way to avoid trouble is to use common sense and deliver exactly what you promise. Nothing more. Nothing less.

WHAT GETS INVESTIGATED?

Many of the mail-order ads you see during the course of a day are breaking the law in one way or another. But there are usually so many violators out there that it takes authorities quite a while to get around to them all. Here are a few of the products, services, and business "opportunities" postal authorities often investigate. Many will sound quite familiar.

- distributorships
- pyramid schemes
- investments
- loans
- dating services
- cosmetics

- weight-loss products
- sexual aids
- real estate
- vitamins and drugs
- franchises

- correspondence schools
- insurance
- securities
- work at home offers
- job opportunities

THE FTC MAIL-ORDER RULE

As the operator of a mail-order business, you'll have three primary responsibilities to your customers—to treat them fairly and courteously, to send them their purchases in a timely manner, and to give them good value for their money.

The Federal Trade Commission has established a number of ground rules governing the relationship between mail-order customers and mail-order businesses. In 1975 it created the Mail Order Rule to address many of the complaints brought against the mail-order industry by its customers. The most common complaint was the amount of time it took to receive merchandise. Many reported never receiving their merchandise at all.

The FTC Mail Order Rule will serve as your guideline for shipping merchandise. If you follow it to the letter, you won't have any problems. It includes guidelines covering a variety of situations.

When you print or mail a solicitation:

- The time period for shipping must be clearly and prominently stated in your solicitation.

- You must have "reasonable basis" for expecting to ship the merchandise within the time period stated in your solicitation.

- If you do not include a time period for shipping in your solicitation, you must deliver the merchandise within thirty days of receipt of the order. *This only applies to orders that contain all the information needed for shipping and for which you have received complete payment.*

If the original shipment date cannot be met:

- You must provide the customer with a notice giving him the option of canceling the order and receiving a full refund or agreeing to a delay in shipment. This is commonly called a delay notice or option notice and must be sent as soon as you realize you cannot meet the deadline. It must include a revised time period in which the customer can expect shipment. It must also state that if the customer fails to respond, it means they are consenting to a delay of thirty days or less.

- If you are unable to give a revised shipping date, the notice must state that fact. It also must state that the order will be automatically canceled unless (1) you ship the order within thirty days of the original shipping date and you haven't received a cancellation notice before shipment, or (2) you receive the customer's consent to the delay within thirty days of the original shipping date. You also must state that they have the ongoing right to cancel the order at any time.

If the revised shipment date cannot be met:

- You must send the customer a second notice, called a renewed option notice, offering them the choice of agreeing to a further delay or to canceling the order and receiving a refund. In this case, however, they must respond in writing to agree to the delay. If you don't receive a response before the first delay period ends, you must cancel the order and send them a refund.

All notices must be sent by first-class mail and should include a prepaid postcard or business reply mail envelope for customers to send you their responses. When you refund a customer's money, it must be sent by first-class mail. If the customer paid by cash, check, or money order, you must send the refund within seven days of the order cancellation. If the customer paid with a credit card, you must credit her account within one billing cycle after the order is canceled.

It's extremely important that you keep careful records of all notices sent and all cancellations. These records are critical in protecting yourself if the FTC should investigate you. They are your only proof that you've complied with the rule. Without them, the FTC can conclude you've been doing business otherwise.

For a complete copy of the Mail Order Rule, contact the Federal Trade Commission, Enforcement Division, Washington, D.C. 20580. Call 202-376-3475.

What Are the Penalties?

There are any number of federal and state agencies whose ire you can arouse if you stray off the beaten track. USPS postal inspectors are authorized to arrest people suspected of violations. The Federal Trade Commission can come after you, as can the Food and Drug Administration and a whole passel of state consumer fraud agencies. You can be charged with mail fraud, false advertising, and a host of other violations. Even the Better Business Bureau can get into the act by alerting the media to your unsavory activities.

What can happen to you? A whole variety of things, ranging from being driven out of business to being thrown in the slammer for a number of years and fined a lot of money (if memory serves me, the feds use mail fraud to get lots of organized crime figures).

The bottom line here is that engaging in illegal or unethical mail-order activities just isn't worth the effort. To operate a business in this manner is unfair to your customers and could result in your prosecution. You can make a good living in mail order without resorting to practices that con people out of their money. If you're not interested in providing a product or service that's commensurate with what you're charging people, find something else to do with your life.

WHAT'S NEXT?

At this point, there's just one thing left to do. Place some ads, send out some mailers, and see what arrives in the mail. You're finally in business and on your way to fun and profit. We'll look at some of the tasks you'll need to do as a business owner in chapter 13.

❦ 13 ❧

FUN AND PROFIT

W e've covered a lot of ground in the previous chapters. A lot of it will help you get started cheaply. All of it will come in useful as you grow your business.

Now it's time to make some money. From this point on, your life will be consumed by your business. You'll have lots of responsibilities and even more worries. Looming above them all will be the bottom line—making a profit. That's what business is all about. It's called running in the black, and here are some of the keys to achieving it.

BE PATIENT

Growing any business is slow work, so if the response to your first ads isn't quite what you were hoping for, don't panic. Stick to your advertising plan and keep beating the bushes. It may take some time for things to get moving. But don't worry. You've done your market research correctly, and you know who your customers are. Once they discover you, things will be fine.

BE AGGRESSIVE

Advertising and promoting your business won't end with your first group of ads. It will be an ongoing effort. Keeping your business fresh in customers' minds is critical to its success.

You'll need to make sure that when they're ready to purchase a product or service that you provide, they'll think of you first. And you can't sit around waiting for customers to find you— you have to go out and get them.

WATCH YOUR ADS

I just want to mention yet again the importance of keying your ads and carefully monitoring the results. When you first place an ad in a newspaper or magazine, you're kind of like a fisherman tossing a lure into a new fishing hole. You may get a lot of bites. You may get nothing.

Remember, in mail order, advertising in the right places is *the* key to success. Pay careful attention to how your ads pull. Stick with those that work well. Get rid of the ones that don't, and quickly. And don't be afraid to try new advertising venues. The world of consumers is constantly shifting. You'll need to experiment a bit to make sure you're reaching all your customers.

SERVICE! SERVICE! SERVICE!

In the highly competitive world of business, success or failure frequently hinges on one simple characteristic—the quality of service you provide your customers. When people buy goods and services today, whether through a retail store or a mail-order business, they can choose from an enormous variety of vendors. They don't necessarily need to come to you. The only way you're going to attract and keep them is to treat them better than anyone else does. For this reason, service has become *the* buzzword for American businesses, from the corner mom-and-pop grocery store to the largest corporations.

Because of the distance and anonymity involved in mail order, service is doubly important. When people order merchandise from you, they expect you to live up to your end of the bargain. Deliver what you promise, when you promise it, and make sure it's worth what you charge.

Good service also requires tact and patience. When you're dealing with the public, you're going to see the whole range of human behavior, from the delightful to the deplorable, and you must be prepared for it. Some customers will be wonderful to deal with, and others will be nightmares. Just remember, you have to treat them all like they're your best customers. No matter how rude, unreasonable, or unpleasant they are, try to send them away happy.

Years ago, when I was in high school, I worked part-time in a store owned by a man who was a clever businessman, but not a paragon of patience. His attitude was "The customer's always right, except when he's wrong," and I saw him get into confrontations with people on a number of occasions. He'd lose his temper and really let them have it, and they'd go away angry and never come to the store again. We lived in a small town where word got around about people, and I knew he was hurting himself. His attitude should have been "The customer's always right, *even when* he's wrong." If it had been, his business would have done a lot better.

Just realize there will be times when you're going to need to put up with a lot of nonsense. Bite the bullet and get it over with. It won't be pleasant, but the alternative can be quite damaging to your business.

GIVE YOUR CUSTOMERS WHAT THEY WANT

Running a business profitably and successfully means constantly fine-tuning your service and your merchandise to meet the needs and wants of your customers. How do you find out what people want? It's simple—just ask them.

After you've been in business awhile, conduct a survey of your customers to see what you're doing right and what you're doing wrong. Insert a business reply card with their merchandise and ask them to take a few moments to fill it out and send it back.

Ask if they're satisfied with the goods or services you provide. Have they been pleased with the speed with which they receive their merchandise? Do they find dealing with your business convenient? Are they satisfied with your guarantees and return policies? Would they make any suggestions to improve things?

Pay attention to their answers. People will usually be pretty honest when they're filling out a survey because of the anonymity involved. If a problem area keeps cropping up, consider yourself warned and take care of it. If there are products they'd like you to carry, try adding them to your selection. If they're unhappy with your service or the quality of some of your merchandise, you'll need to make sure the proper adjustments are made.

YOU'RE IN CHARGE, SO BE IN CHARGE

One of the reasons you're going into business for yourself is you want to be your own boss. But in the process, you may eventually become the boss of several other people as well. As any business owner will tell you, managing employees is sometimes a lot harder than managing customers. Here are a few hints.

BE A ROLE MODEL

Being in charge begins with being in charge of yourself. As the owner of the business, you'll set the tone for your employees. If you show up every day looking down in the mouth or grumbling about your problems, your mood is going to infect your entire staff. You must be upbeat, leave your personal problems at home, and keep a cheerful face on things.

For some people, this is one of the most difficult aspects of being in charge. The business owner who's blessed with a sunny disposition is fortunate indeed. But few of us are happy all the time, and you'll need to learn to force yourself to be good humored even when you're not in a particularly good mood. It can be even more difficult for someone who's thoughtful and quiet by nature. Someone who wants your attention can misread thoughtful and quiet as disinterested and rude. It won't be easy putting a smile on your face all the time, but after you get used to it, it'll become more natural, and you'll find yourself becoming cheerful out of habit.

Learn to Delegate

One of the hardest lessons for most entrepreneurs to learn is they can't do everything themselves. This lesson is just not part of their emotional makeup. They're take-charge people who know they can do everything better than everyone else and don't feel a job has been done right unless they have done it themselves. That's the quality that makes them successful. But it can also keep them running in too many directions at once, wasting a lot of time on trivial things.

Learn to delegate. It's a key to maintaining your sanity. If you've hired responsible people, there's no reason not to trust them. There are just too many little tasks in running a business to try to do them all yourself. If you learn to delegate, it'll give you more time to devote to the really critical jobs that contribute to the success and growth of the business.

Train Your Employees

You may read this and go, "Duh, like I *wouldn't* train my employees?" Well, let me ask you something. Have you ever walked into a store, a restaurant, or some other business and encountered an employee who just doesn't have a clue about how to do their job? If so, did you ever go back to that business again?

It's clear that a lot of people fail to train their employees adequately, despite the fact that poorly trained employees can do irreparable harm to a business. Make sure yours know what's expected of them and are trained to meet their responsibilities. You can't be there every minute of every day, so they need to know how to handle any and all situations.

Teach them how to deal with customers and handle complaints. Train them in the use of the computers and inventory control systems. Post important phone numbers next to your telephones. Make sure your training is thorough, and do it *before* you turn them loose without supervision. On-the-job training is effective, but it can create inconvenience for your customers.

BE A GOOD BOSS

Being an employer is an awesome responsibility. It should be taken with the utmost seriousness. When you hire someone, that person is dependent on you for his livelihood and the well-being of his family. Before he retired, my father ran a small manufacturing company that had around forty employees. The one thing he always talked about was his concern for his employees and how he felt the weight of that responsibility more than any other.

It's a tough job. Just as your customers will show you every facet of human behavior, so will your employees. Some will be hard workers who are self-motivated, can think on their feet, and will go beyond their normal area of responsibility to make sure that things get done right. Others will be drones who only move when they need to and won't be able to function outside the narrow focus of their job descriptions.

You'll get the full range of personalities, too. Some of them will be happy and outgoing, the type of people who make wonderful salespeople or waitpersons or any other job where close customer contact is required. They'll get along with you and your other employees and will be positive factors in your business. Others will turn out to be morose, self-pitying whiners who only see the negative side of things. They may be difficult to get along with and can be a potential negative factor in your business. They'll require a lot of training and attention.

SOMETIMES YOU NEED TO BE KIND

Being an employer requires wearing many hats—psychologist, den mother, cheerleader, referee, and sometimes dictator. You'll need to be keenly attuned to your employees' emotions and problems and go out of your way to accommodate their needs. You'll have employees who go through divorce, illness, the death of a loved one, psychological difficulties, and all the other events we experience in the normal course of our lives.

You'll need to bend over backward to help your employees through their difficult times. If you're successful in fostering a sense of family, it will help enormously. Next to a person's real family, his work family can be a great source of emotional support in a time of crisis.

Sometimes You Need to be Tough

You're also going to have employees who, for one reason or another, just don't work out. They may be lazy, show up for work irregularly, be rude to customers or other employees, or just plain be incompetent.

Your first responsibility is to help them correct their behavior. Sit them down, explain the problem, tell them what they need to do to correct it, and give them a few weeks to see if it works out. If it doesn't, you must fire them.

You're also going to have employees who are dishonest and ripping you off every time your back is turned. In this case, fire them as soon as you have documented proof of their dishonesty.

In both these cases, the firing must be handled delicately. Prepare a letter stating why the person is being let go, and present it to him at a meeting. If you are worried that the employee may be emotionally unstable, arrange for another person to be with you. If you have any doubts at all about your legal rights to terminate an employee, consult with your attorney before you take action.

EMPLOYEE OR INDEPENDENT CONTRACTOR?

You'll recall from chapter 4 that one of the 12 Rules For Doing It Cheaply is don't hire employees. It's much cheaper t people as independent contractors and let them worry about their own taxes and insurance.

The IRS has taken a hard look at the employee versus independent contractor issue and established criteria defining each one. Here are some of the ways it distinguishes between the two.

In general, *employees* are workers who:

- are required to comply with instructions about when, where, and how they are to work;
- are trained by other employees and are required to attend meetings and other company functions;
- provide services that are integrated into company functions;
- are required to render their services personally;
- work a schedule that's determined by the person hiring them;
- devote full time to the work, are told how much time they must spend working, and are told whether or not they can do work;
- perform their work on the premises of the person who is paying for the work;
- are told in what order their services must be performed;
- submit regular or written reports;
- are paid by the hour, week, or month;
- receive reimbursement for their business and traveling expenses;
- are furnished with tools, materials, and other equipment;
- can quit without incurring any liability;
- can be fired;
- have a continuing relationship with the person hiring them.

ral, *independent contractors* are workers who:

the facilities and equipment used in performing ce;

- realize profits and/or losses;
- perform services for multiple unrelated firms at the same time;
- make their services available to the general public on a regular basis.

These criteria are not carved in stone, but they can serve to give you a general idea of how the IRS looks at employees and independent contractors. The bottom line is they prefer people to be considered employees and will do all they can to define someone as such. If you have questions about the status of someone you intend to hire, check with your accountant or other tax expert *before* you hire that person.

PAY YOUR TAXES

You'll also need to be honest in dealing with Uncle Sam. When you're self-employed, you have to take on the responsibility of making sure your taxes are paid on time. That means sending in a quarterly statement of estimated tax to the IRS, and possibly to the state, to cover your tax liability for the year.

If you have employees, you'll also be responsible for withholding a portion of their pay for prepayment of their taxes. You'll also need to withhold their half of the social security tax, or FICA. The other half of the FICA payment will come out of *your* pocket. There will be other withholdings for state income tax and disability insurance.

These payments are due quarterly, so you'll need to make sure the money's on hand. The best way to do this is to open an interest-earning account with your bank and use it specifically for withheld taxes. Put the proper amount of money in the account every payday *and leave it there.* You may be tempted to use it for something else, telling yourself you'll pay it back by the time the quarterly payments are due. Don't do it. If you fall behind in your payments, the IRS can seize your business and conduct an auction of its assets to get the money you owe them. You can face severe penalties, too.

YOUR FUTURE

By now, I hope you've learned that mail order will be one of *the* growth industries in the 21st Century. I hope you've also learned that starting a mail-order business requires careful planning and research. Take your time and look carefully at potential products. Evaluate their markets, both for today and for the long term. Examine demographics, social trends, and other factors that will affect the market for the product. Test the product's marketability and make sure it will earn you the income you need. Once you're convinced it's the right product, put together a solid business plan and get the nuts and bolts of your business ready to go. When everything's ready, it'll be time to place that first ad.

Successful entrepreneurs not only recognize business opportunities before the rest of the world, they make sure they know what they're doing before they take the leap into business. You need to do the same. Think of success as a wonderful place that's visible to you on the other side of a deep gorge. The only way to reach it is to build a strong bridge. That bridge is your business, and it requires the same careful construction as a real bridge.

Build your business carefully, and you'll enjoy success, profitability, and the pleasures and rewards that come with working for yourself. If you choose a good product, work hard, and keep an eye to the future, you'll never regret your decision.

❧INDEX❧

Accountant
  CPA (Certified Public Accountant), 141
  hiring of, 140–41
Address, for mail order business, 116
Advertising, 153–78
  catalogs, 171–73
  classified ads, 157–58
  comic books, 176
  cooperative mailings, 176–77
  direct mail advertising, 164–71
  display ads, 159
  do-it-yourself aspects, 154–55
  faxed ads, 162–63
  information sources on, 177
  inquiry-and-follow-up method, 159–60
  on Internet, 163
  of Internet site, 190–92
  keying ads, 163–64
  on matchbook covers, 174
  to motivate customers, 155–56
  radio advertising, 161–62
  stuffers, 175
  Sunday newspaper inserts, 175–76
  take-one advertising, 174–75
  television advertising, 160–61
  and understanding of customers, 155
Advertising costs, 67

Answering machine, home-based business, 124
Attorney, hiring of, 140

Baby boomers, profile of, 20–21
Banks, choosing bank, 141–42
Becker, Frank, 6
Books, sales volume of, 29
Break-even-point, computation of, 100
Business cards, 117
Business plan, 54–55, 143–52
  cash flow calculation, 149–51
  contents of, 54, 55
  cover page, 145
  description of business, 145
  financial information, 145–46
  information sources on, 152
  and loans, 54, 74–75
  management structure, 145
  market analysis, 146
  marketing strategy, 146
  plan of operation, 147
  start-up cost calculation, 147–49
  timetables/schedules, 147
  value of, 143–44
Business reply mail, 207
Business structure, 131–38
  incorporation, 59–60, 136–38
  information sources on, 142
  partnership, 133–35
  sole proprietorship, 59, 131–33

Cash flow
  analysis for business plan,
    149–51
  and payment methods, 59
Catalogs, 171–73
  and new business, 172
CD-ROM drive, 127
Classified ads, 157–58
  market testing with, 105–6
  and pricing of items, 158
Clothing, sales volume of, 28
Collectibles, sales volume of, 29
Comic books, ads in, 176
Communications industry, deregu-
    lation of, 196
Compact discs/tapes, sales volume
    of, 29
Competition
  and global economy, 3
  and market testing, 101
  and pricing product, 97
  and service business, 8
Computer literacy, and small busi-
    ness owners, 40
Computers, 125–29
  basic software, 128–29
  buying guidelines, 126–28
  CD-ROM drive, 127
  going online, 63
  MAC versus PC, 126–27
  modem, 127–28
  necessity for small business,
    62–63
  and printers, 128
  and scanners, 128
  surge protector, 130
Consignment, selling on, 83
Consumer behavior
  and ideas for business, 77–78
  motivations for buying, 78–81
Cooperative mailings, 176–77
  types of systems, 176–77

Cover letter, direct mail package,
    169–70
Crafts, sales volume of, 29
Creativity, and small business own-
    ers, 35–36
Credit cards
  financing business with, 73
  and mail order business, 24–25
Cultural diversity of population, 22
Customer satisfaction, 202
  good service, importance of,
    226–27

Decision making, and small busi-
    ness owners, 35
Delegation, importance of, 229
Demographics
  baby boomers, 20–21
  cultural diversity of population,
    22
  elderly population, growth of,
    22
  and product evaluation, 91–92
  rising birth rate, 21
  single-parent households, 21
  two-income family, 20
Direct mail advertising, 164–71
  cover letter, 169–70
  and mailing lists, 165–68
  order forms, 170–71
  postage for, 172–73
  promotional literature, 170
  reply envelope, 171
Discipline, and small business own-
    ers, 35
Display ads
  characteristics of, 159
  market testing with, 106
Downsizing
  examples of, 304
  and growth of small businesses,
    2–7

Drop-ship arrangements, 82–83,
    201–2
  advantages of, 201–2
  disadvantages of, 202
  operation of, 83

Elderly population, growth of, 22
Electronics, sales volume of, 29
Employees
  versus independent contractors,
    56–57, 231–33
  IRS criteria for, 232
  training for, 229–30
  withholding taxes, 233
Entrepreneurs
  characteristics needed, 34–44
  entrepreneur potential quiz,
    45–50
Equipment
  answering machine, 124
  computer, 125–29
  fax machine, 124–25
  telephone, 123–24
Existing business, buying business,
  9–10, 88–89
Express Mail, 206

Fads, versus long-term sales,
  92–93
False advertising, 220
Families
  adjustment to new business,
    43–44
  baby boomers, 20–21
  for financing business, 72
  single-parent households, 21
  working in new business, 44
Faxed ads, 162–63
Fax machine, 124–25
  basic features, 124–25
  combined with printers/copiers,
    125
Fax/modem, 125, 128

Federal Express, Web site, 194
Federal Trade Commission (FTC)
    Mail Order Rule, 221–23
Financial management, and small
    business owners, 41–42
Financial services, sales volume
    of, 27–28
Financing business
  from credit cards, 73
  determining initial costs, 66–68
  from friends relatives, 72–73
  from home equity loans, 69–70
  information sources on, 76
  from life insurance policies, 74
  and living expenses, 68–69
  from partner, 71
  from sale of personal items, 72
  from savings, 55–56, 60–61, 69
  from severance packages, 72
First-class mail, 206
Flexibility, and small business
    owners, 38
Flyer
  for market testing, 104–5
  simple, construction of, 104–5
Focus groups, 102–4
  questions for, 103–4
  sample of product for, 103
  selection of members, 102–3
Fourth-class mail, 207
Franchise, 10–11, 89
  advantages of, 10, 89
  disadvantages of, 11, 89
  fees related to, 11
  growth of industry, 10
Free gifts, with purchase, 156
Furnishings, for home office,
  129–30

Gifts, sales volume of, 28
Global economy, and competition,
  3

Goal orientation, and small business owners, 38–39

Health
consumer interest in, 78–79
and small business owner, 44
Hispanic population, growth of, 22
Hobby, turning into business, 52–54, 82
Home-based business, 6–7
answering machine, 124
benefits of, 6–7, 119–20
computer, 125–29
disadvantages of, 120–21
fax machine, 124–25
insurance, 130–31
and lease restrictions, 119
office furnishings, 129–30
office in, 122–23
office supplies, 130
versus renting space, 55
telephone, 123–24
and zoning laws, 118–19
Home equity loans, 69–70
shopping for, 70
Home-shopping networks, 161
Housewares, sales volume of, 28
How to Start and Operate and Mail Order Business (Simon), 14
How-to publications, 82

Ideas for business, 77–95
checking catalogs, 85
checking magazines/newspapers for, 84–85
and consumer behavior, 77–78
consumer motivation for buying, 78–81
drop-ship arrangements, 82–83
hobby/interests, 52–54, 82
Internet selling, 86–88
mail order from existing retail business, 85–86

retail to mail order transition, 85–86
self-production of product, 81–82
selling on consignment, 83
single product business, 81
traditional-type product, 83–84
vintage products, 88
Illegal activities, 219–23
common fraudulent products, 220–21
false advertising, 220
lotteries, 220
obscene materials/pornography, 219–20
penalties, 223
pyramid schemes, 219
Incorporation, 59–60, 136–38
advantages of, 59–60, 136–37
disadvantages of, 137
incorporation fees, 59
ownership of business, 136
S corporation, 138
and taxation, 137–38
Independent contractors
versus employees, 56–57, 231–33
IRS criteria for, 232–33
Informational publications, 82
Inquiry-and-follow-up method, 159–60
disadvantage of, 160
examples of, 159
Insurance, home-based business, 130–31
Internet, 63, 179–97
advantages of Internet business, 189–90
advertising on, 163, 190–92
creating Web page, 163, 185–87
customer base, 192
growth of, 183

(Internet cont.)
Internet business, example of, 87–88, 183–85
interruption of service, 192–93
large companies on, 179–80
links on, 191
management of, 183
monthly costs, 187, 193
orders/payments, receiving on-line, 188–89
origins of, 180–82
renting connection on, 187, 193
selling on, 87–88
server for Web site, 187–88
service providers to, 182–83
shipping merchandise, 193–94
start-up costs for business, 194–95
Inventory, 66–67
inventory control, 204–6
minimal, benefits of, 58, 204
turning over inventory, 204

Learning, consumer interest in, 80
Lease, and home-based business, 119
Legal factors
information sources on, 142
product evaluation, 94–95
Legal Pot, 92
Leisure time, consumer interest in, 79
Liability
avoiding, 60
factors in product evaluation, 94–95
and incorporation, 59–60, 136–37
Life insurance policies, financing business with, 74
Limited partnership, 135
Living expenses, determination of, 68–69

Loans, 56
and business plan, 54, 74–75
Logo, design of, 117
Lotteries, 220

Magazine co-op mailings, 177
Magazines
ideas for mail order product, 84–85
sales volume of, 28
Mailing lists, 30–33, 165–68
brokers for, 166
buying lists, 165–66
buying versus renting list, 167
creating from customers, 168
effectiveness of, 32–33
negative aspects of, 167–68
targeted populations for, 31–32
by zip codes, 168
Mail order
convenience factor, 15–17
and FTC Mail Order Rule, 221–23
growth of industry, 11–12, 15
historical view, 23–26
laws regulations related to, 24
scope of merchandise offered, 26–30
versus shopping, 17–20
Mail order business
address for, 116
advertising, 153–78
benefits of, 12
business plan for, 143–52
business structure for, 131–38
financing of, 65–76
ideas for business, 77–95
illegal activities, 219–23
information source on, 14
on Internet, 179–97
inventory control, 204–6
market testing, 101–12
name for, 114–17

(Mail order business cont.)
  order processing, 198–204
  pricing products, 96–101
  product evaluation, 89–95
  shipping, 206–18
Mail-order co-op mailings, 177
Market for product
  demographic factors, 91–92
  evaluation of, 90–91
  long-term versus fads, 92–93
  niche market, 91
Market testing, 101–12
  with classifieds, 105–6
  and competition, 101
  with display ad, 106
  with flyer, 104–5
  focus groups, 102–4
  ongoing testing, 112
  response rates, computation of,
    106–11
Markup
  on mail order products, 97
  on retail products, 97
Mass customer co-op mailings,
  177
Matchbooks, ad on, 174
Modem, 127–28
  fax/modem, 125, 128

Name of business, 114–17
  business cards/stationery, 117
  idea generation for, 115–16
  logo for, 117
  and long-term, 115
  registration of, 116
  simplicity for, 114–15
Niche market, 91
Nostalgia, consumer interest in,
  79–80

Obscene materials/pornography,
  219–20

Office equipment, saving money
  on, 61–62
Optimism, and small business owners, 39
Order forms, in direct mail package, 170–71
Order processing, 198–204
  customer names on master list,
    200
  drop ship arrangement, 201–2
  opening/sorting mail, 199–200
  preparation for shipment,
    200–201
  recording orders, 200
  record keeping, 202–4
  shipping, 201, 204–18
Outsourcing, meaning of, 4
Overhead, and pricing product, 98

Package delivery services, 25
Partnership, 133–35
  advantages of, 133, 134–35
  disadvantages of, 71, 135
  for financing business, 71
  limited partnership, 135
  and taxation, 135
  Uniform Partnership Act,
    133–34
People-orientation, and small business owners, 40–41
Personal items, selling to finance
  business, 72
Pet Rock, 77–78, 92
Postal business centers, 207–15
  listing of, 208–15
  services of, 207–8
Pricing product
  adjustment of price, 99–100
  and break-even-point, 100
  and competition, 97
  markup, 97
  and overhead, 98

(Pricing product cont.)
  pricing formula, 98–99
  and product characteristics, 97
  and target sales volume, 98,
      99–100
  and unit cost, 97–98
Printers, for computers, 128
Priority mail, 206
Product evaluation, 89–95
  investment factors, 90
  legal factors, 94–95
  market for product, 90–91
  niche market, 91
  seasonal factors, 93
  shipping factors, 93
  suppliers, 93–94
Professionals, hiring of, 138–40
Profits, reinvesting in business,
      60–61
Promotional literature, in direct
      mail package, 170
Pyramid schemes, 219

Radio advertising, 161–62
  per inquiry deal, 162
Record keeping, for orders, 202–4
Renting space, versus home office,
      55
Reply envelope, in direct mail
      package, 171
Retail business, 8–9
  benefits of, 8
  disadvantages of, 8–9
  going mail order with, 85–86
  selling on Internet, 87–88
  start-up, 8–9
Role model, business owner as,
      228–29

Savings, financing business from,
      55–56, 60–61, 69
Scanners, 128
S corporation, 138

Sears & Roebuck, 23
Seasonal products, 93
Second-class mail, 206
Self-improvement, consumer inter-
      est in, 80–81
Service business, 7–8
  benefits of, 7–8
  disadvantages of, 8
  start-up, 7–8
Service economy, 5–6
  growth of, 5
Severance packages, using to fi-
      nance business, 72
Shipping, 201, 204–18, 206–18
  as factor in product evaluation,
      93
  and FTC Mail Order Rule,
      221–23
  and Internet business, 194
  overnight services, 194
  postal business centers, 207–15
  U.S. Postal Service, 206–18
Shopping, disadvantages of, 17–20
Simon, Julian L., 14
Single-parent households, increase
      in, 21
Small businesses
  appeal of, 1–2
  buying existing business, 9–10,
      88–89
  entrepreneurial self-analysis for,
      34–50
  franchise, 10–11
  home-based businesses, 6–7
  reasons for growth of, 2–7
  retail business, 8–9
  service business, 7–8
  and service economy, 5–6
Software, basic types needed,
      128–29
Sole proprietorship, 131–33
  advantages of, 131–32

(Sole proprietorship cont.)
  disadvantages of, 132–33
  and personal liability, 59
  and taxation, 133
Specialty co-op mailings, 177
Sporting goods, sales volume of, 28
Start-up costs
  and business plan, 54–55
  calculating for business plan, 147–49
  computers, 62–63
  evaluation of, 42–43
  home office versus renting space, 55
  incorporation fees, 59
  for Internet-based business, 194–95
  inventory, 58, 66–67
  minimum, examples of, 51–54
  office equipment, 61–62
  savings, use of, 55–56, 60–61
  for workers, 56–57
  See also Financing business
State name abbreviations, 217–18
Stationery, 117
Stuffers, 175
Success, consumer interest in, 80–81
Sunday newspaper inserts, 175–76
Suppliers, reliability of, 93–94
Supplies, for home-based business, 130
Surge protector, 130

Take-one advertising, 174–75
Target sales volume, and pricing product, 98
Taxation

employee withholding, 233
  and incorporation, 137–38
  and partnership, 135
  quarterly payments, 233
  and sole proprietorship, 133
Telephone
  custom features, 123–24
  home-based business, 123–24
  toll-free number, 124
Television advertising, 160–61
  effectiveness of, 161
  expense factors, 161
Third-class mail, 206–7
Toll-free number, 124

Uniform Partnership Act, 133–34
Unit cost, and pricing product, 97–98
UPS, Web site, 194
U.S. Postal Service, 206–18
  business reply mail, 207
  Express Mail, 206
  first-class mail, 206
  fourth-class mail, 207
  postal business centers, 207–15
  priority mail, 206
  publications of, 216–17
  second-class mail, 206
  state name abbreviations, 217–18
  third-class mail, 206–7

Vintage clothing, 88

World Wide Web, 63
  See also Internet

Zip codes, mailing list by, 168
Zoning, 118–19
  zoning categories, 118–19